A FEDERATION OF
SOUTHERN AFRICA

A FEDERATION OF
SOUTHERN AFRICA

LEO MARQUARD

LONDON
OXFORD UNIVERSITY PRESS
CAPE TOWN   JOHANNESBURG
1971

Oxford University Press, Ely House, London W. 1

GLASGOW NEW YORK TORONTO MELBOURNE WELLINGTON
CAPE TOWN SALISBURY IBADAN NAIROBI DAR ES SALAAM LUSAKA ADDIS ABABA
BOMBAY CALCUTTA MADRAS KARACHI LAHORE DACCA
KUALA LUMPUR SINGAPORE HONG KONG TOKYO

ISBN 0 19 215644 6

PRINTED IN GREAT BRITAIN
AT THE UNIVERSITY PRESS, OXFORD
BY VIVIAN RIDLER
PRINTER TO THE UNIVERSITY

FOR
TAMAR, GARTH
AND ALAN

PREFACE

THE purpose of this book is to examine the possibilities of federalism in southern Africa. It is by no means a blueprint for federation, and it has been my endeavour throughout to avoid distracting attention from the main purpose by intruding details that can rightly only be discussed when the general principle has achieved some measure of popular approval. Some detail is unavoidable if the discussion is not to remain in the air, but this has been kept to a minimum.

I wish to thank my friends Monica Wilson and Quintin Whyte for having suggested to the Rhodes Trust that it should make it possible for me to spend some five months in Oxford—and, of course, to the Trust for having acted so generously on the suggestion.

The Master and Fellows of St. Cross College invited me to become a Visiting Fellow for the duration of my stay at Oxford, an honour which delighted me as much as did their excellent company. My wife and I were fortunate enough to be able to live in Queen Elizabeth House and are grateful to the Warden and staff for this and many acts of kindness.

I am indebted to my friend David Welsh for reading and re-reading the manuscript and for making stimulating suggestions and discussing them with me.

Finally, it is strictly true that the manuscript would neither have been begun nor finished but for the encouragement and critical appreciation of my wife.

L. M.

Claremont
February 1971

CONTENTS

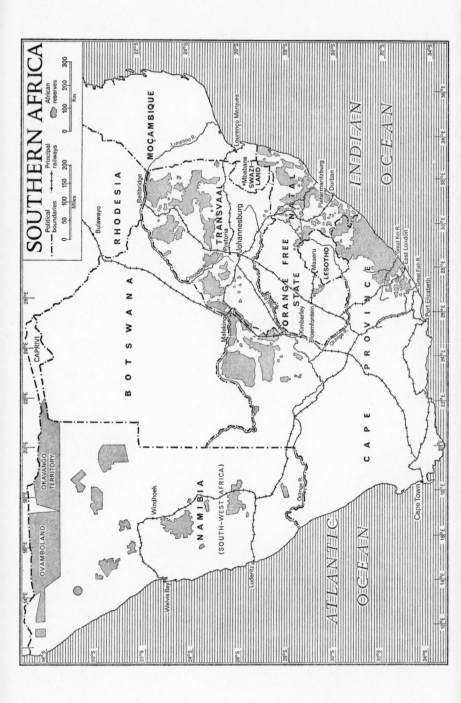

1

THE PRESENT DILEMMA

THE internal race policies of the Republic of South Africa appear to be leading inevitably to stagnation or to a collision between white and non-white, which would be bloody and solve nothing. To a native of South Africa this is not a happy thought. But the word 'inevitable' has no real meaning in human affairs except in the sense used by the American who 'always compromised' with it, when, of course, it ceased to be inevitable. It is therefore necessary to try to find out whether, if the appearance is indeed real, there are not alternative practicable policies that might avoid both dangers.

Though mankind constantly blunders into violence and then glorifies it, men and women prefer order to violence, and peace to war, and have shown ingenuity and ability in constructing political systems that make it possible to have what they want. That such systems do from time to time break down is proof of nothing more than that, like all human institutions, they are imperfect and have failed to make the adjustments required by a changing society. Making such adjustments is a complicated business, because although society is not static, human beings seem to become more conservative with age and resistant to change, particularly in the machinery of government and the laws and customs to which they are accustomed.

The policies of those who wield political power and the system of government they use to implement them, react on each other. Sometimes the policies dictate what the system should be and at others the system favours the adoption of particular policies. When the road a country is taking seems to be leading to disaster—and both stagnation and violence must be so regarded—it is possible that the policies only are at fault. Change the policies, some people say, and all will be well. In the opinion of other people it may be only the machinery of government that has failed to keep pace with changing circumstances. It is, however, much more likely that policies and the system of government have interacted and both must be examined if we seek alternatives to the threatened disaster. In regard to the Republic of South Africa we must first ask whether this threat is in fact real, for if it is not it would be unnecessary and mischievous to meddle with existing institutions.

The words 'good' and 'bad' are not really appropriate in speaking of government and governmental institutions. 'Good' tends to be that of which the speaker approves. Nevertheless, it is difficult to find more suitable words to express some of the ideas contained in the following paragraphs, and there is in fact a fairly large area of agreement about their meaning. Most people would agree about the goodness or badness of a country judged by such things as its economic growth, the distribution of wealth, education and social welfare, its transport system, the integrity of its administration. They would agree in general that it is good to have security, prosperity, and peace. Disagreement usually begins in considering the ways in which these objectives are attained and the price to be paid for them, which, it must be noted, are not reckoned in simple economic terms. In 1940 there were those in Britain who believed that peace and security might be attained by surrendering to Germany. That is what Hitler offered. But in the opinion of the great majority of the British people it would have meant the peace of the grave, and security bought at the cost of liberty. This price they were not prepared to pay and they accepted the enormous economic sacrifice that they knew their choice would entail. There were, no doubt, people in Britain who believed that liberty was a fine thing but that war and insecurity were too high a price to pay for it. They were in a minority.

Take a rather more complicated example. Many people regard individual liberty and the rule of law which protects it as two of the most important concepts of Western civilization and they believe that any government that abrogates the rule of law is bad. In Western Europe there is today a general acceptance of this view even in countries where the liberty of the individual is flouted. Yet in a racially mixed country such as South Africa, where political power rests with a white minority descended from Western Europe and heirs to its traditions, many whites disagree with this. They believe that liberty and the rule of law are important but that they can be bought at too high a price in a multiracial society. They argue that Africans had, traditionally, no conception of democracy or of the rule of law and that it is dangerous folly to apply such alien ideas to them. It would not be difficult to show that such views rest on inadequate knowledge of pre-white African social and political history and institutions, but this will not do much to convince people who have been persuaded that a government is bad, not when it abrogates the rule of law, but when it insists on upholding it in all circumstances. In this case, a majority of white South Africans believe that the price of liberty and the rule of law is their own personal safety and political power. This price they are unwilling to pay and, since liberty is indivisible, their own liberty must be curtailed. This is one of the things that the 'contemporary ancestors' in Europe of white South Africans find it most difficult to understand; and it would be naïve of the white rulers of the RSA to expect that the way in which they exercise their power will be judged by different standards from those that apply in Western Europe. According to those standards the government of the RSA is bad.

There is still great argument in South Africa and abroad about her race policies, but nobody disputes that it is those policies that set her apart. Particular aspects of her government may, when judged separately, receive general approval. Her system of transport, the standard and volume of production, industrial legislation for white workers, economic rate of growth, these may mostly be assessed in statistical terms and she may be judged to be a good field for investment. Her system of administration, achievements in the field of sport, her scientific and economic expertise may all be of acceptable world standards. But her race policy permeates every other policy. Every law that is passed has an inherent racial aspect, and all social, economic, and political life is based on race policies. The RSA may be an excellent trading partner; she is financially strong, she pays her debts, and constitutes a good market. Judged by these things she is a member of the international community in good standing. But it is on her race policies that she will continue to be judged, and to find what effect her policies generally are having on her international relations we need look no further than her race policies.

The basic facts of South African history, from which these policies have sprung, are that whites conquered the country from non-whites and used their position of strength to entrench their political power. As a result, that power today rests with some three and a half million whites, and the sixteen and a half million non-whites have no representation in any of the councils of the nation that matter. The details of this conquest are interesting, moving, and often heroic, but for our present purpose need not detain us. Until the middle of the twentieth century it was essentially the same story in many parts of the world: infinitely better equipped—economically and scientifically—white people from Europe conquered the indigenous people of Africa and entrenched themselves in their position of privilege.

From the end of the Second World War, however, the story takes a new turn. Privilege became suspect, particularly when it was related to skin colour. Where, in previous centuries, European nations had scrambled to conquer and 'own' as much of the non-white earth as possible, they now scrambled to disburden themselves of what had become embarrassing colonial possessions. In one territory after another the metropolitan power granted independence, often too hastily and without sufficient thought to what happens to the subject when a colonial ruler/subject relationship is suddenly severed.[1] There were, however, a few places where the whites had struck firm roots and no longer had a home country to withdraw to. South Africa was one such place. At the very time that whites elsewhere were, willingly or reluctantly, disengaging themselves from their colonial subjects, white South Africans were entrenching their privileges still more deeply despite the increasing volume of protest from the rest of the world.

The decolonization movement took the world and South Africa unawares. Within two decades, hundreds of millions of former colonial subjects became independent and their white rulers either stayed on in advisory capacities or in business, accepting the fact that they were no longer privileged masters, or they packed up and went 'home' to Europe. White South Africans too had some millions of 'colonial subjects', but both they and their white rulers knew only one home—South Africa itself. White South Africans could not go home as the British and French were free to do; and they were unwilling to regard their colonial subjects as equals. They had, therefore, two alternatives: to continue ruling non-whites as if nothing had happened or to grant them some measure of self-government, holding out hopes for their ultimate independence. Since coming to power in 1948 the Nationalist Party has tried both alternatives at the same time.

In retrospect, it was a forlorn attempt to govern as if nothing had

[1] It has been generally believed that no group ever voluntarily surrenders power. The decolonization operation after the Second World War seems to be, at least, a partial exception. For the severing of ruler/subject relationship see Mannoni, *Prospero and Caliban*, London, 1956.

happened. After all, a very great deal has happened since the Second World War. The world had become colour conscious and could never be the same again. The conception of a master/servant relationship based on colour could no longer be supported in theory; and in practice it could be maintained only by enforcing legislation of a kind that had itself become abhorrent to the western and the eastern world alike. Discrimination based on colour might survive in various parts of the world but it was no longer a tolerated or respectable way of life. This was the way of life that the South African government, with white electoral support, set about maintaining.

The general term for the body of legislation that exists to maintain white power and privilege in South Africa is apartheid, a word that has passed into the English language and is no longer printed in italics. Much of that legislation was on the statute book before the Nationalists came to power, but they sharpened the definition of the general policy and added many new laws and regulations. These are not essentially Nationalist Party or South African, but are characteristic of a society in which a small white minority has achieved political power through self-government before the large non-white majority is either ready for or has been granted direct representation in a central legislature. Indeed, they are not even essentially white colonial but are characteristic of any society anywhere in the world in which a small minority holds sway. Such laws regulate the movement of the majority, in this case the non-white Africans, Asians, and Coloured; they control the recruiting of labour and the movement of people from rural areas to towns and industrial cities; and, generally, they impede the mobility of labour, though, as long as there is no shortage of labour, this has little economic repercussion. Strikes by non-whites are prohibited and trade unions inhibited; to avoid 'unrest', the right of peaceful assembly is restricted and protesters given short shrift. Since social mixing would weaken the whole structure of apartheid, social separation is necessary, and where it is not already customary it is prohibited or discouraged by law. Land laws make it illegal for people of one race to acquire or occupy land in an area designated for another race, and the amount of land so reserved for whites is out of all proportion, qualitatively and quantitatively, to their numbers. Other laws, prompted partly by humanitarianism, provide for separate education and for medical and other social services for non-whites, invariably on a much inferior scale to those for whites. These are the crumbs of social legislation. The history of the world, East and West, has many examples of these methods by which a minority in power controls a majority. They are by no means confined to domination by one race over another, and they are certainly not confined to South Africa, but this does not make them any more acceptable. What is perhaps peculiar to the South African situation is that such methods are increasingly anachronistic.

It is characteristic of such discriminatory laws that the penalties for breaking them become increasingly severe. New laws are constantly called for by those in charge of security to stop loopholes and discourage further protest. Authoritarian regimes have to take increasing dictatorial powers to protect their authority. Freedom of speech and of writing, free assembly, the right to organize peacefully in defence of group interests or of individual rights and liberties, have all to be curtailed, and if the courts are too zealous in maintaining the rule of law and protecting liberty, they must be excluded from the operation of administering such laws. All this is to be expected. In 1948 there were in South Africa organized African, Asian, and Coloured congresses and other bodies that were outspoken in defence of their rights. There were also many individual whites and a few interracial bodies that not only sympathized with non-white aspirations but actively supported them in defending their rights. Clearly, if that kind of activity had been allowed to continue unchecked, it would have undermined apartheid and greatly reduced the chances of maintaining white supremacy. Any non-white organizations that criticized the country's race policies seriously had to be suppressed; white or mixed bodies received special attention from the security branch of the police; banning organizations and individuals, without any obligation to give a public reason, became frequent; fear of losing a passport or of failing to get a permit was freely used to induce conformity; and year by year fresh legislation would give a minister or someone designated by him powers to arrest, to ban, to silence and, when necessary, to exclude the courts from taking cognizance of such ministerial action. This was one of the two paths that South Africa followed.

The second alternative open to the white people of South Africa, since they were unwilling to share political power with non-whites, was to grant them some measure of self-government. In this matter the government had an instrument to hand in what is known as the

Bantu Reserves. These are areas where African tribes were living when they were conquered by the whites and which they continued to occupy; but the boundaries of tribal areas had been much shrunken by conquest and today all the tribal Reserves put together constitute less than fourteen per cent of South Africa. Since the nineteenth century it had been Native policy to recognize tribal chiefs and customs and to rule the Reserves through tribal institutions. After 1948 the government developed this policy considerably. The Reserves were then designated Bantu homelands and the policy gradually came to be to grant them some measure of local self-government with the implication, sometimes explicitly stated, that these homelands would become self-governing—and eventually independent—Bantustans. Tribal institutions were still used where possible, but the principles of Western democracy could not be withheld from Africans who had become familiar with them, and popular elections became part of the machinery of local government.

There are in the nature of things close limits imposed on such a policy. The homelands, constituting less than fourteen per cent of South Africa, are unable even in the most favourable circumstances to bear more than some forty per cent of the African population; the rest will continue to live and work in white areas where they can never have the normal rights of citizenship and where their presence is at the will of white authorities. Even if all the political and economic obstacles could be overcome and, against all odds, five or six viable Bantustans brought into being, the white rulers in their areas would still have to decide whether or not to share power with the non-whites. Moreover, it is highly improbable that white South Africa would concede genuine independence to the Bantustans, because to do so would endanger white security. So far from solving any problem for the white rulers such a policy would aggravate it, because Bantustans could so easily become foci of discontent for those Africans within the white areas who would still be living under discriminatory laws. As it is, the RSA is maintaining a far greater army than she needs to ward off possible external aggression. The existence of independent Bantustans would increase the pressure for larger armed forces.

As far as Africans are concerned, the Bantustan policy does at least base itself on the reality of land. There are actual tribal homelands, however fragmented and inadequate they be. For the Coloured and Asian population there is no land that could be regarded as

B

'their own'. Group areas, based on colour and race, have been established in urban areas, but they do not constitute a 'national home'. For both Coloured and Asian the furthest that 'self-government' can go would be the creation of artificial local councils and of an elected national council without any territorial basis.

All the tentative steps already taken by the white rulers of the RSA along the alternative road of granting self-government to some of the non-whites, show one thing clearly: this road must come to an abrupt end. That is the point where there is either collision or stagnation.

Just as practically all the legislation in South Africa flows from the desire to maintain white rule, so her relations with foreign countries are coloured by that desire—coloured in the eyes of the world, and because of that in her own eyes. This is true of both unofficial and official contacts. Inside Africa she maintains diplomatic relations with her immediate neighbours—Lesotho, Botswana, Swaziland, Rhodesia, Malawi and the two Portuguese territories of Angola and Moçambique; but no other state in Africa desires diplomatic links with the RSA. Outside Africa she has diplomatic relations with all the more important countries except communist China and Russia, though she trades with these countries, and India and Pakistan. By UN resolution, member states may not supply arms to the RSA unless they are purely for defence against outside attack. This resolution has not been fully carried out by all members of the UN, but apart from buying arms South Africa trades freely with most other countries, and one of the main functions of her department of foreign affairs is to promote trade. Though it is difficult to get information on the subject, there is possibly a disguised but greatly limited trade between the RSA and India, Pakistan, and a number of African states that have, in theory, broken off trade relations. At the official level, then, South Africa's diplomatic relations with many foreign countries are friendly, in the strict sense that they are not at war; but they can hardly be called cordial. When the Prime Minister visited parts of Europe in 1970 he was cordially received in Lisbon and Madrid, but there was some evidence that his visit embarrassed the French Government, and that he would have been unwelcome in Holland had he expressed a desire to visit this country which has had the oldest links with South Africa.

It is at the supranational level of the UN and its agencies that she has experienced the full force of world opinion against apartheid.

In the UN Assembly there have been a number of well-nigh unanimous resolutions concerning South Africa's race policies and calling
upon her to alter her laws; and in the Security Council she has been
saved only by those countries, such as Britain, who while strongly
disapproving of apartheid, agree that this is an internal matter about
which the UN is precluded by its Charter from acting. South Africa
continues to enjoy co-operation on the World Bank, the Atomic
Energy Agency, the International Monetary Fund, and several other
international bodies. But although, as a member state, she is entitled
to take part in the conferences and activities of all UN agencies, she
has been virtually excluded from some of the most important, such
as the World Health Organization, the Food and Agricultural
Organization, and the International Labour Organization. This is
usually achieved by the refusal of delegates from African and Asian
states to listen to the South African delegates and their threat to walk
out rather than sit in the same conference. It is regrettable that South
Africa should be thus excluded, for she has much to contribute to the
general good; but it is part of the price paid for her policies that she
is precluded from much fruitful international co-operation.

While South Africa's friends were able to put up a case for her at
the UN for non-interference in her internal affairs, it was more
difficult to do so in regard to the ex-German colony of South-West
Africa. The international status of that territory has not been finally
established. In 1919 South Africa was made responsible to the League
of Nations, through the Permanent Mandates Commission, for the
administration of South-West Africa under a C Mandate. After the
Second World War South Africa asked the UN for permission to
incorporate the territory. This was refused, and so began the long
dispute between South Africa and practically the whole of the rest
of the world represented at the UN, where South Africa's claims
were strenuously denied. In 1961, two member states, Liberia and
Ethiopia, both former members of the League of Nations, tried to
test the matter in the International Court at The Hague. The case
dragged on for five years when the Court, by the casting vote of the
President, gave the negative verdict that Ethiopia and Liberia had
no *locus standi* except as parties to a dispute. While South Africa
hailed this as a victory the rest of the world did not regard it in that
light. Indeed, the South African Government itself admits that, while
not abating her claim, the status of South-West Africa is different
from that of a South African province. Nevertheless, South Africa

maintains that she has the right to govern the territory, as she is in fact doing, and to apply all the laws in force in the RSA to it. The vast majority of states at the UN maintain that the country should either be administered under a trusteeship agreement or else be independent, and in anticipation of this latter solution, South-West Africa has been named Namibia. The uncertainty[1]—for so it remains —about the status of South-West Africa enables the UN to discuss South Africa's race policies under the heading of South-West Africa. In these debates her race policies are freely condemned, but that does not alter the fact that she occupies the territory and could, presumably, be removed by force only.

It is perhaps at the unofficial level that the impact of world opinion on South African whites has been greatest. There is hardly a branch of sport—certainly of major sport—from the international participation of which South Africa has not been excluded or threatened with exclusion because her teams are selected, not on merit only, but on grounds of colour. Where her teams are still invited to visit another country the matches take place under police protection and in an atmosphere of unrest because of well-organized mass protests that frequently end in violence. This happened to her rugby tour, in 1969–70, of Great Britain and Ireland; and long before a cricket tour was due to start in 1970 there were massive threats that the games would be disrupted and counter threats against the disrupters. The Prime Minister of Britain, other Ministers of the Crown, bishops, university dons and students, and other leading men and women expressed opinions on what had clearly become a burning public question: should the MCC invite a team, selected according to the principles of apartheid, to tour in Britain? Opinions were divided, but a few days before the tour was due to start the general excitement had reached such a pitch that the Prime Minister asked the MCC to reconsider its invitation, and the tour was called off. In the field of sport—cricket, rugby, athletics, football—South Africa's isolation is on the way to becoming complete.

In other fields where international contact is usually regarded as valuable there have been boycotts or partial boycotts against the

---

[1] Early in 1971 the International Court at The Hague convened in response to a request from the Security Council of the UN for an advisory opinion on the legal implications for member states of the continued presence of the RSA in Namibia. Whatever this opinion turns out to be, it would be unlikely to alter materially the fact that South Africa is in physical possession of the territory and would not voluntarily abandon it.

RSA. It has become increasingly difficult to attract good university teachers, and South Africa is not always welcome at international conferences where non-white university men and women are, as a matter of course, taking part. Playwrights, actors, and authors are among those who have signed letters and statements protesting against one or other of South Africa's laws or administrative actions, such as refusing a passport to Alan Paton or Athol Fugard[1] or the banning of a book by Nadine Gordimer. Some have refused to appear on the segregated stage in South Africa or to have their works performed there. In some cases South Africans have themselves committed the act of exclusion from world organizations. The three largest Afrikaans churches, for instance, so much resented criticism from fellow Christians abroad that they cut themselves adrift from the world body. And the South African Government, of its own accord, withdrew from UNESCO because it could not accept that body's views on racial equality and freedom.

The result of such boycotts is spiritual and cultural isolation to which grave penalties are attached. It produces spiritual and cultural impoverishment and, worse still, the belief that this does not matter. As boycotts tighten and isolation increases, South Africans of all colours are thrown back on their own resources and will end, not only by comforting themselves that this does not matter but by believing that it is really all to the good. The final stage is to believe that anyone who disputes this is unpatriotic. In matters of industry it could be argued that isolation would be a good thing because it would force South Africa to produce more of her own manufactures. This is a spurious argument. Applied to matters of the mind it is a dangerous delusion. When South African writers and artists and scientists—not to mention sportsmen—are no longer able to measure themselves and their achievements against the best that exist in the world, standards must fall.

It is not only white opinions that are relevant to the policies being followed by the RSA. One of the most serious aspects is the hardening of non-white attitudes. Fifty years ago African and Coloured leaders were willing and anxious to co-operate with whites in working out policies. But non-white leaders and congresses, essentially moderate at the beginning, became increasingly radical as their efforts to achieve some say in government were rebuffed. As they became more radical they appeared more 'dangerous' to whites, so

[1] Alan Paton's passport was restored to him in 1970 and Athol Fugard's in 1971.

more legislation and more force was used to counteract what the white rulers regarded as a threat to stability and security. This process of thwarted moderation turning to radicalism is familiar enough in history. In the RSA it has gone to lengths that threaten to exhaust whatever goodwill between whites and non-whites there may still be.

It is the ways described in the preceding pages that lead to isolation and stagnation—or to a collision. And this is the way along which South Africa's race policies are leading her. It is the way along which there are no alternatives. An examination of the effects of those policies at home and abroad makes this clear, and the danger signs are clear for all to read: a precarious racial 'peace' maintained by security police and increasing arms and by violence done to Western concepts of law; growing international antagonism; and an apparently buoyant economy showing symptoms of decline. And at the end of the road—stagnation or violence. But if there is no alternative along that road there may yet be another road. There are indeed other roads and it has seemed to me that the road of federation might offer the greatest hope.

2

THE MEANING OF FEDERATION

THIS is not a book about the theory and practice of federation. On that subject there are many excellent works. Nevertheless, since I propose in subsequent chapters to examine the possibilities of applying the principles of federation to southern Africa, it would be as well to explain briefly what, in this context, is implied by the word federation. This is the more necessary for two reasons. The word has come to have unfortunate connotations, particularly in Africa, where it tends to be regarded as a kind of political trick to ensure the continuance of white domination, and so delay the advent of freedom for colonial subjects. Unless this impression can be erased, discussion of federation in southern Africa will be bogged down in prejudice. In the second place there has been so much detailed study of federalism in recent years that the word has become at once over-defined and more extensive in its application. On the one hand, writers have tended to deny the term to constitutions that deviate in some minor fashion from a supposed norm. On the other, there is a tendency to discover the 'federal principle' at work in almost every form of government and, indeed, of human organization. For the purpose of explaining the practical advantages and disadvantages of constitutional federation to the people most concerned—those who, if it is embarked upon, will have to live with it—a more flexible and less all-embracing account would seem to be necessary.

In broad terms, a federation is a system of government in which power to make and administer laws is divided between a central authority and a number of unit authorities which may be called provinces or states, and are in fact the territories that joined to form the federation. For the purposes of this discussion the terms 'central' and 'regional' will be used throughout. One further point should be made at once: it is assumed that the federating regions are all governed on a broad democratic basis. It would be an amusing academic exercise to discuss the possibilities of a federation between states ruled democratically and those in which a dictator held power; but for practical purposes it would be a waste of time.

In a unitary form of government all legislative power resides in a central parliament which normally delegates authority to make ordinances to regional authorities; but this in no way impairs the sovereign power of the central authority. What immediately distinguishes a federal system from this is that, in the former, sovereign powers are divided between central and regional authorities. In a unitary system parliament is sovereign. In a federal system there is, strictly speaking, no sovereignty except that which resides in the constitution; but it is sometimes convenient to speak about central and regional governments each having certain 'sovereign' powers that were allocated in the act of federating.

Federations are made when a number of regions, as Dicey put it, 'desire union but not unity'. The people of those regions may believe that it will be an advantage in such matters as defence, trade, or banking to present a united front to the world, but they may wish to retain their autonomy for cultural and other reasons. They will then have to decide which subjects of legislation are to be allocated to the central authority and which to the regions. In some cases such decisions are comparatively straightforward. For instance, we would be inclined to say off-hand that the central authority should have control over such matters as peace and war, defence, and communications. But what about education or trade within a region, or agricultural marketing? As we shall see later, there are many factors that might influence people in coming to decisions on such matters.

The division of powers may be made by drawing up a list of all known subjects on which legislation may be required and dividing them in one of two ways: certain specified subjects allocated to the central authority and all the rest to the regions; or specified subjects to the regions and everything else to the centre. A third way is to specify the subjects for the centre and also those for the regions. Whichever way it is done, however, there will always remain those matters which do not call for legislation at the time the federation is being made, but which may very well do so at some time in the future. For instance, few people a century ago would have supposed that legislation would ever be called for to control air traffic. Powers to legislate on such unforeseen subjects are called residuary powers, and in the third way of federating mentioned above it will have to be decided where the residuary powers are to go—either to the centre or to the regions. In the first two methods the residuary powers are, of course, included under the terms 'all the rest' and 'everything else'.

Which of these four ways is selected by people of regions wishing to federate will depend on many local factors. This will be discussed later. But whatever way is chosen, cases are bound to arise where the constitutional rights of the regions conflict with those of the central authority. It is therefore essential in a federation to have legal means of settling such disputes, and this is a function of a supreme court. A unitary state may have a written or an unwritten constitution, but parliament is sovereign and the supreme court cannot question an act of parliament, though it can decide that a so-called 'act' was passed without observing all the required constitutional steps. In a federation, the supreme court has the special function of interpreting the constitution and thus of deciding issues of conflict between a region and the central government.

When a number of regions decide to form a unitary state they vest the sovereign powers formerly possessed by them in a central authority. This is done by a formal constitution which can, thereafter, be changed by the central authority. But when regions form a federation and divide sovereign powers between the central and the regional governments, the constitution cannot be changed by such simple means as an act of parliament. There are a number of 'sovereign' parliaments, no one of which can, by itself, alter the contract under which it entered the federation. Yet there must be some way of altering the constitution when changed circumstances demand it. It must not be impossible to change it, but it must not be easy. To meet this need, federal constitutions provide that the constitution may be amended only with the agreement of, say, a majority of two-thirds of the votes in three-quarters of the regions.

These then are the main characteristics that distinguish a federal from a unitary constitution. There are, of course, many more differences, but they flow from these three: a division of powers, the special function of the supreme court, and the machinery for constitutional amendment.

It is worth while looking at a few of the existing federations to find out what the conditions were that made the inhabitants of the regions decide that it was both safe and useful to federate. Primarily, of course, and to go back to the broad definition of federation, it was because they believed that their interests would be served by joining with the other regions but were unwilling to give up *all* their independence. Perhaps the question ought, therefore, to be differently framed: what special factors existed that persuaded the regions that their interests would be served by associating with other regions? Why could they not go on happily as in the past?

In rather general terms there are divisive and cohesive forces at work in any given area.[1] Examples of the first are the existence in that area of groups that want to maintain their individuality, as, for instance, with strong group nationalism, or tribalism, to which it is akin. Another disruptive force may be the breaking up of empire, when things fall apart. Strong religious or cultural convictions may also be divisive. On the other hand, industrialization and urbanization, that do not depend on tribal units, operate as cohesive forces. The growth of an educated élite, too, anxious to play a part on the international scene, might be cohesive because it requires the use of a world language, such as English or French, which may conflict with a national language and its divisive tendencies.

Professor K. C. Wheare studied the federations of USA, Australia, Switzerland, and Canada and found that the following factors were present in each case:[2]

1. A feeling of military insecurity and a desire for common defence.
2. The realization that independence of foreign powers could be attained only by combining.
3. The hope of economic advantage.
4. In each case the federating communities had had some political association, even if it was only that they had been governed by some outside power.
5. Geographical contiguity.
6. Similarity of political institutions.

Although it is sometimes asserted that federations are not possible unless there are strong cultural interests in common, neither race nor language nor religion are included among the factors above. In actual fact, if all six factors are present the existence of strong cultural *differences* may well be the factor that decides people to want

---

[1] See U. K. Hicks and others, *Federalism and Economic Growth in Under-developed Countries*, London, 1961, pp. 13 et seq.

[2] K. C. Wheare, *Federal Government*, second edition, 1952.

a federation rather than a closer union. It should be noted, too, that neither is the list of factors exclusive nor can federation not be achieved if they are not all present.

Having analysed the factors making for federation, Wheare went on to find out why the people of those areas did not want closer union but preferred federation. He listed the following factors:

1. The federating regions had all had a previous separate existence.
2. They regarded their economic interests as divergent in some respects: for instance, though an industrial and an agricultural region might find certain economic interests in common, they might yet desire final control over other economic interests.
3. While geographic contiguity was necessary for some kind of union, great geographical distances and differences in climatic conditions might be arguments against closer union.
4. Differences of race, language, religion, or nationality.
5. Dissimilarity of social institutions: for instance, as in the United States, where there was a difference between slave and free states, or in Canada where the difference was between French and English civil law.

Once again the list is not exclusive. Since 1952, when Wheare published his book, new factors have entered into the situation and some of those he listed may no longer be of great importance. Of the six listed by him the desire to be independent of a foreign colonial power is hardly relevant in a political sense, though it may still have considerable economic significance. Insecurity from outside threats has been profoundly modified by modern weaponry and by the international line-up of great powers. On the other hand, the motive of economic advantage has probably been increased by the advent of new techniques of mass production, of marketing, and of capital mobilization from which a small state cannot hope to reap full advantage. In other respects the incentive is much greater to combine than when the federations studied by Wheare came into existence.

There is one new factor that is particularly relevant in discussing former colonial territories in Africa, and that is race. When the so-called classic federations, such as the USA and Canada, were established in the eighteenth and nineteenth centuries power rested entirely with white colonists and it hardly entered their heads to regard non-white subjects as possible future citizens. To most people the 'colonies' consisted of white people who ruled over non-white, and when constitutions were made or regions decided to federate it was whites who both took the decisions and shaped the constitutions and federations in their own interests. Non-white opinion was seldom considered.

Since 1948 all this has changed with a bewildering rapidity and it is today almost inconceivable that the making of any kind of constitution in Africa will be undertaken by whites only; indeed, in most African states it is black Africans who would effect any constitutional changes that might be needed. The abortive Central African Federation during the fifties illustrates this. White Rhodesians wanted a federation and the British Government so far bowed to the new ideas flooding through Africa as to consult their African subjects in what were then Nyasaland and Northern Rhodesia. It was indirect consultation by officials and, as far as can be ascertained, African opinion was massively opposed to a federation which would, they feared, bring them under white Rhodesian rule. Nevertheless the federation was proceeded with and, almost inevitably, failed. In the end the only way in which the whites in Rhodesia were able to produce a constitution of their own was to break away from Britain and declare themselves a republic, which the rest of the world, however, refused to recognize as independent.

The first factor mentioned by Wheare as inducing people to want federation was insecurity from an outside threat. This is the factor that is the most profoundly influenced by new attitudes about race. Those attitudes may well give white rulers in states such as Rhodesia or the RSA an even greater sense of insecurity, a greater fear of attack from outside. Moreover, the sense of insecurity may be increased in two ways: the white ruling minority might fear that an external enemy would find a sympathetic non-white population within the country; or it might fear that, if a dissatisfied non-white population revolted, it would receive support from external sources. Such fears might sharpen the desire for federation as an escape from an intolerable situation. This question will be dealt with more fully later.

Meanwhile, there are a few other aspects that should be examined by those who are considering a federation of the regions in which they live. It was assumed, earlier, that the federating regions are all governed on a broad democratic basis. This remark needs to be expanded. Democratic government implies, in very general terms, that the legislature is elected by the people and is, from time to time, held responsible by them through popular elections. It implies that an alternative government can be established without revolution; and this in its turn implies freedom to organize for constitutional replacement of those in power. Such freedom is safeguarded by law and by an independent judiciary. There are two main ways in which the executive arm of government is formed. In the USA the head of the executive, the President, is elected by popular vote for a fixed period of four years and he appoints his cabinet. Neither he nor his chief executive officers are members of Congress. In Britain, the leader of the strongest party at a general election becomes Prime Minister and chooses his ministers. He and they are all members of parliament. There are, of course, many other differences between a constitutional monarchy and a presidential-type democracy, but for our present purposes it is sufficient to say that, in forming a federation on a democratic basis it does not matter which of the two forms is chosen provided the principles of constitutional replacement of government, the rule of law, and the independence of the judiciary are maintained.

There is a further proviso: the constitution must embody a bill of rights. When the thirteen American states federated they did not include such a statement of individual rights and liberties; but they soon found it necessary to remedy this, as they did by the fourteenth amendment to the constitution. The rights and liberties of the individual are always in danger from executive government whose agents find it simpler and more expeditious to ignore them. This is not because the agents are by nature authoritarian but, usually, because consideration of individual rights frequently does delay action. Freedom of speech, of conscience, and of movement; freedom from arbitrary arrest and imprisonment without public trial; the right of access to the courts of justice—these are among the liberties that governments sometimes find it convenient to ignore. The danger of this is increased by the growing complication of modern government and by the tendency, already noted, to centralize power. It is greatly increased by a prolonged life-and-death war when the security of the state must take precedence over the rights of the individual. After five or six years of such centralizing of authority, people and governments alike grow accustomed to it and authoritarianism threatens to take over. The way to avoid this, of course, is for citizens to be vigilant in defence of their own liberty. In this they will be greatly assisted by a bill of rights, constitutionally entrenched, and guarded by an independent judiciary.

It is natural that people, when considering the application of federation in their own regions, should look to existing models. There are plenty of these and many books have been written describing them, and in some cases analysing them to find out whether they have 'failed' or 'succeeded', and why. Caution should be exercised, however, not to accept uncritically the reasons why the federation of the United States, for instance, may be regarded as successful when the original constitution was a failure. We are apt to argue that mere continuance of existence—mere survival—is a sign of success and break-up a sign of failure. How, in any case, are success and failure measured? It has been said that the Founding Fathers of the United States had two objectives: to defend its citizens both against external aggression and against internal tyranny. To what extent has the United States been 'successful' in the second objective? American Negroes and Red Indians might give a different answer to this question from that advanced by most white Americans. Moreover, the newer federations that were established during the break-up of colonialism have existed for too brief a time for adequate analysis and valid conclusions. Some of them have actually fallen apart and may therefore be said to have failed. But people seeking a federal union of a number of regions need not necessarily regard those federations that have broken up as models to be rejected entirely. Even federations that have broken up may provide useful pointers. The post-war federations had many special factors to contend with that were absent when the older federations were established. In Africa, particularly, it is not yet possible to say with any degree of certainty what the effect of rapid disintegration of colonialism and the severing of colonial relationships has been.

We do know that a colonial relationship is one of psychological dependence of subject on ruler, and when it is severed there are somewhat unpredictable results for both—unpredictable and disturbing.[1] In the second place, colonial boundaries in Africa were often drawn without any consideration of the inhabitants of the area. Tribes were cut in two, one part belonging to Britain and the other to Portugal or some other country. This thoughtless destruction of the inner coherence of tribal life left problems of government with which white rulers could cope because their rule rested, ultimately, on force. But

[1] See Mannoni, *Prospero and Caliban.*

the newly independent African states were thus left with problems that had been submerged rather than solved by the colonial governments, and resurgent tribalism has been one of the most intractable of post-independence problems. Finally, the last stages before independence saw the emergence of a strong nationalist party intent on hurrying the process, by force if necessary. In the nature of things there would have been no opposition party, and when independence arrived there was one powerful party ready to take over the government. This tendency towards one-party states was hard to resist, but it greatly complicated constitutional development on democratic lines.

Granted the desire of a number of regions to federate, it is improbable that they will find an exact model for what they are seeking. They can, however, find great advantage in studying those trends that are to be found particularly in the older federations, and might possibly be regarded as danger signals. For instance, there is a tendency in the USA and in Australia for the central government to become stronger at the expense of the regions. This may be due, in the first place, to war. During a total war power gravitates to the executive and, within the executive, to a small number of people who have to make big decisions quickly. In a unitary state this means that the prime minister and a small inner cabinet take decisions; in a federal state it will be the president and executive of the central government to whom extraordinary powers will be granted by the regions. It would not be surprising if, when the danger of war had passed, the executives were reluctant to divest themselves of powers which had enabled them 'to get things done' in an emergency.

Another reason why power tends to gravitate to the centre is peculiar to what is called the welfare state—and all modern states are to a greater or lesser extent welfare states. Economic depressions, unemployment, and the needs of social services that are not of a local nature, are possibly best dealt with by central direction. It is doubtful if such large-scale social undertakings as the New Deal in the USA could have been carried through without centralizing authority. Someone remarked recently that no country that was famine-prone should be in a federation because the only effective way of organizing famine relief was by a strong central authority. He was, of course, slightly overstating the case; but his point is clear enough. What it comes to is that the modern state must perform functions that were not thought of a century or two centuries ago and that, to perform those functions, power must to some extent be centralized. In the USA this process has been aided by decisions of the Supreme Court in cases in which state and federal rights were in conflict.

In this matter, too, we should be careful not to regard such centralizing of power as unique to federations. In unitary states all power rests with the centre in any case; but in both England and France, for instance, many decisions have in the past been taken at the local level, either by tradition or for administrative convenience. In recent times, however, strong centralizing tendencies have been noticeable in both those countries. It is a modern phenomenon rather than a characteristic of federations. Here, too, we should not be too quick to draw conclusions about tendencies in any particular federation.

Federalism is sometimes advocated by those who believe, with some justification, that individual liberty is more secure under weak and decentralized governments—and they see federations as essentially weak and decentralized. There is no validity in this argument. In modern federations the central government may well be growing stronger at the expense of regions, but as we have seen, strength and centralization are not synonymous. What is important is that in the federations political power is dispersed and this dispersal cannot be vitally altered without constitutional amendment. Herein, possibly, lies greater security for individual liberty in a modern state.

Some writers regard it as characteristic of a federal state that there is a dual citizenship—a loyalty to the region and to the central authority. This is so. A federation is a union of people as well as of territories, and individuals will regard themselves as, for instance, both Virginians and citizens of the USA. There is nothing novel about this. The citizens of Virginia will have legal and tax obligations both to Virginia and to the Federal government and will help to elect representatives to the state and to the federal legislatures. Unless there is a civil war, however, this dual loyalty will not be a divided loyalty in any material sense. Moreover, in unitary states individuals have strong local loyalties—a Worcestershire man may even regard Kent as a 'foreign' country whose hops should not be brought freely into his own county. As in a federation, such a man has legal and tax obligations locally and centrally, the main difference being that there can, in a unitary state, be no legal dispute between the central and the regional authorities. By tradition—which is very powerful—Whitehall will be cautious about overriding local feelings and prejudices; but that does not give the regional authorities any sovereign powers, as in a federation.

Probably the most complicated and delicate question that arises in considering federations is that of financial arrangements between central and regional authorities. Regions are likely to differ in economic resources between densely populated industrial areas and thinly populated agricultural or forest lands. The industrial—and, more so, mining—regions are able to tax much more heavily than the government of an agricultural region. On the other hand, it is possible that an otherwise economically poor region may possess some strong economic asset, such as a natural harbour or the headwaters of a river that can be harnessed for power, which would be of great value to the mining or industrial state. Indeed, it may even be that the mining state cannot exist effectively without such an asset. That would be a happy state of affairs because each region would then have a strong incentive to co-operate with the other and a strong bargaining counter with which to enter negotiations.

Even supposing that a number of independent regions believe that it will be to their general advantage to federate, the question of financial arrangements may yet prove a stumbling block. It is sufficient, at this stage, to mention some of the issues involved. Since the central and regional authorities in a federation each have sovereign powers to legislate on agreed matters, it follows that each authority must have unconditional control over the finances required to carry out its functions. Each authority, central and regional, must therefore have the power to tax. But the amount raised by taxation in an economically poor state may be insufficient for what has to be done. This problem arises, of course, in a unitary state and is met by some variation or other of a grant-in-aid from the government to the local authorities. In a unitary system, however, the central government makes the grant-in-aid and, in general terms, fixes the amount and controls the expenditure. In a federation this would be contrary to the whole conception of federation, in which powers are divided. If there is to be some kind of grants-in-aid—and it is not possible to avoid them—these must be set up in such a way that they do not depend on the goodwill, annually expressed, of the wealthier regions. They must, in fact, be laid down as part of the constitutional agreement, so that each region receives its share of the national cake as of right and not as an act of charity.

An arrangement of this kind is bound to be viewed with suspicion

C

by the wealthier regions in a proposed federation. Their citizens are likely to argue that they will be asked to pay for the social amenities of the poorer regions. If, for instance, the large revenue from mining in one region is to go to a central fund from which each region draws an agreed percentage, the taxpayers of the mining region will ask why they should be taxed for the benefit of other regions. This is a pertinent question and it is the kind of 'hard fact' question that should, and certainly will be, asked when proposals for federation are considered. The answer lies in showing that the general economic *and other* advantages of the federation in question balance, or may even outweigh, the disadvantages that citizens of the wealthier state may feel. If such an answer is lacking the federation is not likely to succeed. Even if it comes into existence, federation based on such an imbalance will falter. For instance, the people of Northern Rhodesia suspected that they were being asked to join the Central African Federation so as to 'pay for Southern Rhodesia'. These suspicions were allayed, but when it became clear that there was no balancing advantage, this fact helped to destroy the federation.

Regions that consider entering a federation with other regions will, therefore, want to assure themselves that their economic interests will not be jeopardized. They will also demand that any distinctive cultural interests they may have will be safeguarded, and these are sometimes, as in the case of religion, more important to people than economic interests. There may, for instance, be considerable economic or defence advantages for a culturally separate people, speaking their own language to which they are devoutly attached, to join in a federation with totally dissimilar regions. If some form of closer association becomes essential, a federation would be the only acceptable form. A unitary association would place the culturally separate people at the mercy of a central government with sovereign powers. In entering into a federal arrangement, such a region would itself be able to safeguard its cultural interests in the constitution.

It is natural that when people are asked to consider entering into a federal agreement they should take thorough account of how their own interests are likely to be affected. And the governments of such independent regions would be neglecting their duties if, at the negotiating table, they failed to protect the interests of the people they serve. A federation is not an amiable arrangement for advancing the brotherhood of man, except in so far as any sensible system of ensuring peace, orderly government, and liberty may be said to do so. When regions consider some form of association the bargaining will be tough and in hard definable terms, rather than ideological. If the association is to have any chance of enduring, it will have, as far as humanly possible, to be formed in practical terms.

This is not to say that so-called hard economic facts are the only ones to be considered. The facts of culture, language, race, and defence may be equally hard and even more stubborn, though they are not definable in statistical terms. It is in all these spheres that, in the establishment of federations that have lasted, leadership has played a vital part. Political leadership is essential from the very beginning—to persuade people that it would be worth while to consider federation. Once that has been done, and local opposition overcome, leaders of the other regions concerned must be approached and it will take political skill and much time to arrive at the conference table. That point will never be reached unless the leaders are themselves convinced of the common sense of federation and have managed to convince a majority of their followers that it is desirable and practicable. If such conviction is lacking, federation had better be left alone.

3

FEDERALISM IN SOUTHERN AFRICA

In the first chapter the perilous nature of the road South Africa is following was shown. The second chapter contained a brief statement of what, in general terms, federalism entails and how a federation differs from a unitary system. It is now time to examine the possibilities of applying the federal principle in southern Africa. Since the Republic of South Africa is by far the strongest state in southern Africa, no discussion that did not begin with her would have much relevance.

The story of how the present boundaries of southern Africa came into existence is fairly well known. It was partly the story of whites from Europe conquering Africans and annexing their lands; and partly of white colonists exploiting their wealth, establishing their homes, and finally resenting the control of a distant government somewhere 'overseas'. Yet a third part consists of the rivalry between European powers about who should control the valuable Cape sea route and, later, the mineral wealth in the interior. Britain won the battle for most of southern Africa and then handed over the control of the Orange Free State, the Transvaal, the Cape Colony, and Natal to the white colonists. They formed a union which in due course achieved dominion status and, thirty years later, became a republic outside the Commonwealth. Three other territories—Basutoland, Bechuanaland, and Swaziland—continued to be African areas governed by Britain, until, in the 1960s, they became independent as Lesotho, Botswana, and Swaziland. South-West Africa had been a German colony and was mandated to South Africa after the First World War. It is still administered by South Africa despite world opinion as expressed at the UN. Portugal acquired and still holds two large colonies on the east and west coasts of Africa, and Britain held three territories lying between them; Northern Rhodesia, Southern Rhodesia, and Nyasaland. Northern Rhodesia and Nyasaland were granted independence as Zambia and Malawi, while Southern Rhodesia proclaimed her own independence without the consent of Britain. While there will have to be reference to the two Portuguese territories and to Zambia, Malawi, and Rhodesia, it is principally with the remaining territories that this book is concerned: the Republic of South Africa, South-West Africa, Lesotho, Botswana, and Swaziland.

During the nineteenth century a number of Dutch-speaking people from the eastern part of the Cape Colony emigrated, in what is known as the Great Trek, and established republics in the interior. Two of these—the South African Republic (or the Transvaal) and the Orange Free State—eventually achieved their present shape after wars and peace settlements between them and African tribes and Great Britain. After 1854 there were, thus, four white-dominated territories: namely, two independent Boer republics and two British colonies, the Cape and Natal.

During the second half of the nineteenth century various attempts were made to repair the breach between the whites that had resulted from the Great Trek. In the 1850s Sir George Grey, governor of the Cape Colony, attempted to federate the four territories, and in the 1870s Carnarvon, Secretary of State for Colonies, tried his hand at it, even going to the length of annexing the Transvaal in order to promote his policy. This attempt ended with the first Transvaal war of independence in 1880-1, and the question of British control rested there until 1896 when Cecil Rhodes and Jameson tried to overrun the Transvaal by what became known as the Jameson Raid. This was a failure but led directly to the Anglo-Boer War of 1899-1902 when both republics were conquered and closer association between what were now four British colonies became not only practicable but urgent.

It is an instructive exercise to apply to South Africa the criteria that Wheare used in examining the four federations of the USA, Switzerland, Canada, and Australia. In 1908 the four countries and their mother country would have had a strong feeling of military insecurity and a desire for common defence. In the second place, the four colonies were thoroughly aware that their independence could come only by combining. Hope of economic advantage was particularly strong because, as separate colonies, the questions of harbours, customs duties, and railway development that would have to cross boundary lines, had all proved particularly difficult to settle. The Cape and Natal held the trump cards in their harbours, but the Transvaal had the mineral wealth and was the main internal market.

In the fourth place, the four colonies had been politically associated
if by no other fact than they were all governed by Britain. Geographical contiguity was there, and, finally, there was a similarity of
institutions that went back to the nineteenth century: the Free State
and Transvaal had been republics with presidential-type executives
while Natal and the Cape Colony were ruled on parliamentary lines;
but all had been essentially democratic—provided always that the
word was applied in the two republics, and to a slightly lesser extent
in Natal, to whites only.

If we compare all this with the factors Wheare lists as determining
why people are likely to prefer a federation to closer union, the result
is equally interesting. The four colonies had all been separately
administered. They certainly regarded their economic interests as,
to some extent, divergent: Natal, the Free State, and the Cape all had
reservations about having their economic interest dominated by the
Transvaal. There were great geographical distances and climatic
differences that, Wheare found, might favour federation rather than
union. There were strong differences of language and nationality
and, in regard to the Cape Coloured population and the Africans
in Cape Colony, of race. So strong was this difference of race that
it nearly prevented union altogether. There was dissimilarity in
social institutions, and though these were not as marked as those
mentioned by Wheare in the United States—the existence of slave
and free states—they were fundamental and were politically expressed
by the constitutional exclusion of non-whites from citizenship in the
two republics.

On the face of it, then, the four South African colonies seemed
ripe for federation rather than for a unitary association. Yet a majority of the leaders in the four colonies decided on a union. It is
important to try to find out what persuaded the leaders to plump for
union and whether those deciding factors are operative today. In
1907 Lord Selborne, the High Commissioner, at the invitation of the
Cape Government supported by the other three, drew up a memorandum which came to be called the Selborne Memorandum.[1] This
is regarded as the document that gave directional movement to the
general feeling with regard to closer union or federation—and it is
interesting to note that for some time the two terms were inter-
changeable in most people's minds and speech. Selborne dealt

[1] The Selborne Memorandum was published in Cd. 3564, *Papers Relating to
a Federation of the South African Colonies*, London, 1907.

extensively with the advantages of agreement on customs and railway tariffs and of the great difficulty of getting such agreement in
the existing circumstances by negotiation, the results of which had
to be taken back and forth to five legislatures for ratification.

Throughout the Memorandum Selborne referred to 'five' British
colonies, thus including Rhodesia. He also suggested that thought
should be given to 'a central national government embracing all the
British colonies and protectorates', but, apart from that, the Memorandum contained little about the protectorates. When it was submitted to the governments of the four colonies for discussion, the
Transvaal accepted its general terms but added that it would be
happy if Portuguese East Africa could be included. In the event this
was not done. Neither Britain nor the Cape and Natal would have
readily agreed to bring Lourenço Marques and the railway line
from that port to the Reef into the picture. That the suggestion should
have been made at all, however, indicates the strength of economic
factors in promoting the conception of closer association.

There was one other question that Selborne dealt with at some
length and that was the desirability of harmonizing what would then
be called the Native policies of the four colonies. The Cape Colony
had a liberal policy which, in the matter of essential rights of citizenship, did not distinguish between the different racial groups. Natal
was far less liberal but, on paper at any rate, non-whites could
obtain the vote. The two Boer republics had specifically confined
citizenship to whites and, when they were defeated by Britain, were
able to insist that the question of non-white franchise should not be
settled in the peace terms but should wait until the two new colonies
had been granted responsible government. As we now know, this
in effect meant that non-whites in the Free State and Transvaal would
not be enfranchised.

We know that now, but when Selborne was writing in 1907 he
and statesmen at the Cape and in Britain were optimistic about the
matter. They believed that the liberalism of the Cape would spread
to the north. Selborne did not, therefore, devote as much time to that
subject as he did to the generally expressed views that a uniform
system of enforcing law and order among the Native people was
essential. He agreed that some uniformity was desirable but he
issued a grave warning:

It would indeed be a hideous error to suppose that the white people of
this country are discharged of responsibility by perfecting an arrangement

for enforcing order among the native population. The mission they have undertaken is of a far higher and more difficult nature than that, and one which calls for the inspiration of the statesman rather than the science of the soldier. If South Africans are minded to beget a race that will stand on equal terms beside those which inhabit Europe, North America and Australia, they will need all the strength which unity among themselves can give.[1]

Selborne believed that the extent of the country militated against closer union and that a federation was preferable. Others thought so too—great distances and historic and economic differences. Members of the Milner Kindergarten,[2] engaged on doing much of the back-room work for a national convention, favoured federation and assumed that South Africa would follow Canada or Australia. Richard Feetham favoured Canada as a model. Lionel Curtis took it for granted that federation was the only possibility.[3]

There were, of course, arguments in favour of union. It was believed it would be more economic, both in terms of money and manpower, to set up one government instead of five. This argument is specious because it could hardly have been believed that the four colonies could all be governed from one centre. Purely from the point of view of administrative efficiency there would have to be considerable decentralization to overcome the disadvantages of great distances, and that decentralization was in the end provided for by the provincial council system by which there are four additional legislatures that do not have any sovereign powers. Another argument was that such a division of powers as was required by federation would entail legal disputes that would harm the national interest. It was believed, too, that the transition from four autonomous states to one would be easier under a unitary system. Neither of these two arguments stands up to examination; both were speculative rather than based on such experience as was available in Canada and Australia.

The more one examines the arguments for or against union or federation in 1908 the more one is struck by two things: the weight of the evidence in favour of federation and the apparent ease with which the supporters of federation abandoned their cause and

[1] Selborne Memorandum, p. 91.
[2] A group of exceptionally able young men, mostly graduates of Oxford University, whom Milner had recruited. Curtis and Feetham were among them, as were Patrick Duncan, John Buchan, R. H. Brand, and Lionel Hichens.
[3] For a full account of this, see Thompson, *The Unification of South Africa*, Oxford, 1960.

accepted union. It is not easy to find a satisfactory explanation of this paradox but several lines of thought suggest themselves. It was pointed out at the end of the previous chapter that, in arriving at an association of a number of regions, much depended on the leadership in those regions. By far the ablest and most active leaders in South Africa at that time were Merriman in the Cape and Smuts in the Transvaal. Other men, such as Botha, Steyn, and F. S. Malan, had more popular authority; but Smuts and Merriman were preeminent at convincing their colleagues who would, in turn, convince the people. Both men had been trained in British constitutional law and had an almost instinctive perference for that type of parliamentary government. Both men, but Merriman in particular, distrusted what they regarded as the Imperial Factor of whose activities they had both had plenty of experience. Merriman disliked Selborne and distrusted Milner's Kindergarten. Both he and Smuts wanted to reduce the weight in South African politics of the Witwatersrand which, at that time, consisted largely of people whose way of life was alien to South Africa.

Merriman convinced Smuts and Steyn that the Imperial Factor would be reduced by either federation or union. But by the time they came to the National Convention he and Smuts had made up their minds that union was preferable to federation. One explanation for this is an example of what frequently happens in human affairs—judgement based upon insufficient or half-understood facts. Sir Henry de Villiers, Chief Justice at the Cape, spent a week in Canada and, on his return to Cape Town, publicly announced that he had became a confirmed unionist. In a press interview he gave as his chief reason that the wide powers of the provincial legislatures in Canada prevented the merging of French and English. No one stopped to analyse this or to find out whether his other reasons were any more valid. Sir Wilfred Laurier advised Smuts to go for a federation; but Smuts preferred Sir Henry de Villiers's week's experience to that of Canada's prime minister.

There was a further example of basing decision on inadequate information. Articles appeared in the *Transvaal Leader* utterly condemning Australian federation and, though two Australian authorities on the subject described them as prejudiced and misleading, the articles appear to have had great influence. Lastly, Smuts had asked R. H. Brand to write to E. W. Thomson, a Canadian journalist, about the question and Thomson replied strongly regretting the decision that had already been taken for union. His words are worth quoting:

it seems to me very possible that you gentlemen in South Africa, so long accustomed to war and tragic troubles, may possibly set too much store on the advantage of centralization, or unification, as a system giving to or fortifying the Principal Power in authority and in ability for quick strokes. . . . May I suggest that you are all apt to, or may be apt to think *like soldiers* in SA, and so, like Generals, value centralization of authority far too much. . . .[1]

It is interesting to note that Thomson uses centralization and unification as synonymous, a common mistake even today though it is now well understood that it is unnecessary to have a federation in order to promote decentralization; nor is it necessary to prefer a union to a federation if a high degree of centralization is thought to be essential. Smuts and Merriman clearly wanted union and the former regarded federalism as 'hide bound', 'rigid', 'unable to develop as time goes forward', '. . . which will lead to civil war as the American constitution did'. When it came to the National Convention, Merriman proposed a unitary constitution and Smuts seconded him. In doing so, Smuts discredited federalism by reference to Australia and America and maintained that South Africa would not be able to 'get out of the net of friction' except on the basis of complete trust, and that could only be achieved by union. Federation was a denial of trust and a shackling of future generations. It left power to the judges and not to the voters and would tempt governments to pack the Bench. Under a unitary system all these evils would be avoided; there would be economic prosperity; the Native question would be uniformly handled; local loyalties would give place to true patriotism. Steyn supported these views, maintaining that the existing boundaries were artificial and would be perpetuated by federation.[2]

Most of these arguments read today like party-political speeches rather than balanced and well-informed political thought. Using hindsight it can be shown that the arguments had, in the event, little substance. But it is not necessary to employ hindsight to realize that Smuts and Merriman were either arguing from scrappy and inaccurate information about federalism, or were rationalizing in order to bolster their conviction that a unitary system was necessary because

[1] Brand Papers, quoted on p. 107 of Thompson, op. cit.
[2] See Thompson, op. cit., pp. 156 et seq.

of the Native Question, as it was then called. Natal favoured federation because she feared that the English language would not be safeguarded under a union. But some of the most respected leaders at the Cape—J. H. Hofmeyr, Bisset Berry, W. P. Schreiner, J. G. van der Horst, and, of course, Olive Schreiner, opposed union for the very reason that Smuts and Merriman wanted it: they saw in federation the only means of safeguarding the Cape common-roll franchise. They lost the battle and the Cape franchise was, in due course, abolished.

The Native question was, thus, a considerable factor in the decisions arrived at by the South African colonies in 1908 and 1909. The evidence suggests that other factors were but superficially considered, with scant attention to such facts as were available from the experience of other federations. It is possible that, had they been more thoroughly understood, such factors might have enabled the federalists to convince their fellow South Africans. Even in regard to the Native question there is more than a suggestion that, as Selborne in South Africa and Thomson in Canada hinted, it was thought of in military terms rather than in those of statesmanship. Nevertheless, however it was regarded, the Native question loomed large in the thinking of those leaders who got their way at the Convention and subsequently persuaded the white people of South Africa to accept their views. One must remember, too, in questioning the wisdom of men like Smuts and Merriman, Steyn and Botha, what the political atmosphere in South Africa in 1908 was. The bitter memories of the Boer War had not died down, and that war had been the culmination of the struggle for power between the Boers and Britain. But the war itself, having many of the characteristics of a war between brother and brother—a *burgeroorlog*—had shown up the futility of the struggle, and there was a general feeling that 'it mustn't happen again'. The depression and hardship that had followed the war were fading. Gold was once more in production and the economy was becoming healthier. There was, almost everywhere, an optimistic sense, not so much of well-being as of convalescence. In that cheerful half-light everything seemed possible and many people were prepared to risk full-blooded union rather than seek humdrum security in a more cautious federalism—a federation which, Smuts said, would show a want of trust.

Change the name Native question and the question remains the same in essence though almost unrecognizably altered in outward appearance. In 1908 few people thought as Selborne did about the future of the Africans. It hardly entered the heads of most people that Africans had rights comparable to those of responsible white citizens. Africans were, in European terms, untutored tribesmen who had to be taught habits of industry (that is to say, to work for the white man) and while doing so, kept under disciplinary codes that were not applicable to whites. In the process of being taught habits of white industry, they might pick up the rudiments of learning; and, of course, as a Christian people white South Africans had a duty to take the Gospel to heathen Africans. Even along such rudimentary lines there were many white South Africans who believed that teaching the blacks was a most dangerous thing to do. They were of course right.

Obscured by the great social distance between white and non-white lay the essential question of how both could live comfortably and justly in their common fatherland. That question remains, but today most people know that it is not answered merely by a 'Native' policy whose main object is to keep Africans in order; that there is no inherent bar to African intellectual and social achievement; and that one people cannot hope to rule over another for ever. If white South Africans did not know this from their own common sense, experience, and humanity, the rest of the world has left them in no doubt about it.

The uniform Native policy that the pre-unionists felt to be so vitally important in 1908 had, fifty years later, become a reality. If one is considering federation for southern Africa, of which South Africa is the major part, native policy would once more be a dominant factor as it was sixty years ago, but it would be called the race question. Then it was the desire for a uniform policy that made people decide on union. Today it may well be the impossibility of maintaining that uniform policy that strengthens the need for federation. The weight of economic, social, and political evidence in southern Africa against apartheid, and world opposition to it, are such that it is in the highest degree improbable that the RSA will be able to sustain her race policies. It is possible that a federal solution might point the way to avoidance of the stagnation or violence that would benefit neither southern Africa nor the world.

The constitution that came into being in 1910, in terms of the 1909 South Africa Act of the British Parliament, was unitary. Sovereign power was undivided and vested in a central parliament consisting of a house of assembly and a senate. The four colonies became provinces with elected provincial councils who chose their own members of the executive to be headed by an administrator appointed by the central government. The provinces were entrusted with powers to make ordinances on specified subjects, notably education other than higher; but ordinances were subject to approval by the government which can, if it thinks fit, alter the legislative powers of the councils or abolish them altogether. Some writers regard the South African constitution as having 'federal elements' in it and, to substantiate this, refer mainly to three provisions in the Act: legislative powers allocated to the provinces; equal representation of the provinces in the Senate; and the entrenchment of the two sections of the Act that provided for the equality of the two official languages and the safeguarding of the Cape common-roll franchise. Since 1910 the powers of the provincial councils have been altered by act of parliament and, of course, their power to tax or to borrow money is entirely subject to government control. The entrenched clauses were proved, during the 1950s, to be no safeguard, and the composition of the Senate was drastically altered during that same decade. Had the 'federal principle' been a reality instead of an appearance, the Supreme Court of the Union would have been able to prevent the infringement of the constitution in regard both to the Cape franchise and the composition of the Senate. As it was, whatever testing powers the Supreme Court may have had in theory were finally disposed of by parliament itself. In 1961 the question of whether South Africa should become a republic was put to a referendum of white voters who decided in favour of it, and parliament accordingly altered the constitution. Had there been a federation such a drastic constitutional change would not have been possible on a small majority, in this case four per cent of the votes cast.

It will be recalled that President Steyn regarded the colonial boundaries as artificial and feared that they would be perpetuated under federation. So they have been—under union and despite abundant evidence both of their artificiality and disadvantages. The boundaries of the four colonies that were about to become provinces had been drawn during the nineteenth century, as the result of war and with little or no regard to economic or even cultural and ethnic considerations. The present inland boundaries between Namibia and the RSA are the result of agreements with Germany during the scramble for Africa; but South Africa's boundary with Botswana resulted from rivalry between Britain and the Transvaal—between Rhodes and Kruger—that left a portion of Bechuanaland (as Botswana then was) in the Transvaal; and the boundary between the Orange Free State and Lesotho, where it was not a natural boundary, was drawn in peace settlements following the so-called Basuto wars. The division of South Africa was not perhaps as artificial as that in many other parts of Africa, but artificial it certainly was, and has remained. So cumbersome has this become administratively that any organization run on sound business lines disregards the boundaries. The great insurance and banking concerns and, more significantly, the government-owned railways have all done so and found that the change made for greater efficiency.

Apart from the external boundaries just mentioned, South Africa had, at the time of union, a number of internal boundary lines that were also the result of wars of conquest and subsequent peace treaties. But while such boundaries could be clearly marked on a map, the territories within them were subject to the Government of South Africa. A certain amount of administrative decentralization was always part of the white policy of ruling African tribes; but the local regions had no sovereign powers. Thus the Transkei, the Ciskei, and Zululand were clearly demarcated areas, while the Sotho, Tswana, Tonga, Ndebele, and Venda were equally clearly recognizable tribes though the tribal areas they inhabited had been fragmented by wars and population movements and could scarcely be recognized as compact areas. In pursuance of its policy of apartheid the government, from 1950 onwards, laid increasing stress on tribal boundaries and on the encouragement of home rule in tribal areas.

The demarcated tribal areas have an important bearing on the question of federation and it is necessary to discuss them at greater length. The government recognizes nine major and minor linguistic groups:[1]

Xhosa:	3,929,922	Tswana:	1,718,508
Zulu:	4,026,082	Sotho:	1,453,354
Swazi:	498,704	Shangaan:	736,978
Bapedi:	1,603,530	Venda:	357,675
Ndebele:	414,641	Other:	317,965
		Total:	15,067,559

All these groups, with the possible exception of the Xhosa and the

---

[1] Figures supplied by the Department of Statistics. The figures (1970 census) are provisional but unlikely to be substantially altered.

Zulu, live in such scattered and fragmented reserves, or homelands, that any form of home rule would be difficult to establish. Nevertheless, these ethnic groups are distinct in language and culture, and to think of them simply as 'Africans' or 'Bantu-speaking people' would be unreal. There are a number of sub-groups that also have distinct languages and traditions but it is difficult to conceive of their being separately administered and not grouped with some kindred Bantu tribe.

The government's policy has been to set up tribal, regional, and territorial authorities in all homelands and by 1970 there were 429 tribal authorities in which a government-recognized chief and council ruled, 47 regional authorities consisting of a grouping of tribes, and 5 territorial authorities comprising a number of regional groups. In only two areas, the Transkei and Zululand, had the policy advanced to the stage where self-government, as distinct from tribal indirect rule, had become possible. Indirect rule, as understood by Cameron and Lugard elsewhere in Africa, included the conception of tribal chiefs and councils and of tribal treasuries. These conceptions have mostly been swept away with the rest of colonial rule in Africa and it is sometimes forgotten that they provided an admirable training ground at the local level for self-government. In South Africa they are still performing that valuable function.

The words self-government and independence are somewhat loosely used to describe the present constitutional position of the Transkei. It is as well to be clear about these things and it may be better to use the phrase 'home rule', though even that overstates the amount of authority exercised by the Transkei legislative assembly and cabinet. Every act in the Transkei is subject to approval by the Government of the RSA. Indeed, in matters of police, justice, and defence the central government in South Africa is in full and absolute control and the Transkei has no representation in that government.

Well over half the Xhosa no longer live in the Transkei, and many of those no longer regard it as home. They are to be found all over South Africa, working in mines, industries, and white-owned farms. It is therefore slightly misleading to speak about so scattered a population group as if it were a coherent whole. The economy of the Transkei cannot support even this reduced population, and unemployment and hunger are permanent features of the territory. What is true of the Transkei is probably even more startlingly apparent in the remaining homelands. More than half the tribal populations live outside the homelands which cannot support them. The homelands could possibly be made viable if two conditions were observed: that the advice of the Tomlinson Commission be followed to spend hundreds of millions of rands to rehabilitate them and make them economically viable; and that the amount of land that constitutes the homelands be increased from its present inadequate 13·7 per cent of the area of the RSA.

There are strong grounds for arguing that the present policy of the Reserves is bound to fail—for a number of reasons. In the first place, though respect for tribal customs and traditions is much stronger among Africans than is frequently supposed or admitted, so-called detribalization can hardly be arrested in a country that is industrializing so rapidly and in which urbanization has gone to such lengths. A money economy and traditionalism do not consort, and it is the latter that will be submerged. Already many urban Africans know no other home and are ceasing to regard themselves as Xhosa or Tswana or Sotho. Where Bantu linguistic difficulties inhibit communication, English takes over as a lingua franca and as an additional detribalizing force. Westernization with all its incentives and advantages is too strong to resist. In the second place, so long as whites have political control, Africans will not easily regain even the meagre representation they had until 1960; and with more than half their population living in white areas where they have no political rights, independence of the homelands becomes impossible because of the security threat that would pose to white rule in the RSA.

I have myself argued[1] that, in all the circumstances, a carefully conducted dereservation of the Reserves would benefit both them and the rest of South Africa and would do away with the specious argument that Africans do not need to be represented in parliament because they have their government in the homelands. Given the premisses on which it rests, this contention that it would be better to do away with the Reserves is still valid. A homeland that is no genuine homeland but an excuse for exploiting a reservoir of cheap African labour is not only not worth preserving, it is a danger to the body politic of the whole of South Africa. If, however, the homelands were extended and rehabilitated, as the experts agree they can be, they could well become secure bases on which traditionalism can adjust itself more comfortably to the new world. No one would wish to deny that the way in which the demands of a modern economy

[1] *The Peoples and Policies of South Africa*, 4th ed., 1968.

have wrenched African tribesmen from their tribal life, and thrust them into industrial urban areas, has dealt ruthlessly with them, taking them from one way of life and leaving the problem of adjusting themselves to another to the hard school of experience. In the process, African family life has suffered to an extent which some people believe may never be repaired. Well-established homelands might well help to heal the cultural wounds that white civilization has inflicted. But to establish such homelands will require not only more land and capital development. Fully independent homelands with their own foreign policies will never be established unless the white rulers of the RSA are completely satisfied that they will not constitute a security threat to white rule. It is possible that some of the grave questions involved in this situation may find an answer in federation.

To assess the possibilities of federation in southern Africa it is unnecessary to take into account detailed demographic facts about each of the territories concerned. Once the stage of inter-state discussion is reached, such information will naturally play an important part and will be prepared and objectively presented by experts. Too much detail here, however, will tend to fog rather than illuminate the issue. All that seems necessary for the present discussion is the knowledge that the RSA is by far the strongest state in southern Africa in such matters as economic infrastructure, capital, productivity, marketing, and general standards of living. South Africa is roughly equivalent in area to the combined area of the four other territories here thought of as possible regions in a federation; her population outnumbers their combined populations by eight to one. It is to these four territories that we must now turn.

4

SOUTH AFRICA'S NEIGHBOURS

SOUTH AFRICA'S four close neighbours which we are here considering are Lesotho, Swaziland, Botswana, and South-West Africa or Namibia, as it is called at the UN. A brief account of these must now be given.

In theory Lesotho is a constitutional monarchy with a parliament consisting of a nominated senate and an elected national assembly. Before the conclusion of the general election of 1969, however, the prime minister of Lesotho, Chief Leabua Jonathan, carried out a *coup d'état*, suspending the constitution and persuading the king, Moshoeshoe II, to go into voluntary and temporary exile. The breach between the king and his prime minister was apparently healed in October 1970 when the office of the king was more closely defined.[1] Under the new oath of office the king undertakes, among other things, to 'abstain from involving the monarchy in any way in politics, or with any political party or group'. At the time of writing (February 1971) there is no firm information about whether the country will return to the democratic system or continue to be ruled autocratically as a one-party state. What follows is based on the assumption that she will return to normal constitutional practice. If she does not, it is hard to see how she can be made to fit into a democratic federal government and the remaining territories would have to proceed without her.

Four-fifths of the area of Lesotho consists of high mountains or steep hills that make soil conservation—a crying need—expensive. The soil is deficient in humus and has for generations been overstocked and overgrazed. By custom, entrenched in the constitution of 1966 by which Lesotho became independent, the land belongs to the nation. It is held in trust by the chieftainship, and while grazing land is common, chiefs and headmen allocate land for cultivation to individuals. This allocation of arable land is in itself undesirable and leads to favouritism. But the worst feature of the land system

[1] See The Office of the King Order, No. 51 of 1970.

is that it hampers individual effort at improving land and makes the combating of soil erosion well-nigh impossible. The land system and the power of the chiefs are entrenched in the constitution and it would be true to say that, as long as that persists, continued soil erosion is assured. It too is, in effect, entrenched in the constitution. It does not seem possible that anything except a radical constitutional change can prevent further deterioration. There is a population of just over one million, which is more than the country can support, and between thirty and forty per cent of adult Basotho are at any given time earning a living on farms and in industry in the RSA.

The people of Lesotho have a history and traditions of which they are justly proud. These date back to the first half of the nineteenth century when the founder of the nation, Moshoeshoe I, showed great skill and wisdom in protecting his own subjects against African and white aggression and in absorbing remnants of tribes that fled before the Zulu or Matebele conquerors. Fearing conquest by the Boers of the Free State Republic in 1871, he appealed to Britain for protection. This was granted but Britain persuaded the Cape Government to assume responsibility. This worked out badly and ended in the so-called Gun War of 1884 when the Basotho refused to obey a government order to hand in their rifles. When the war was over, Britain resumed responsibility and Basutoland remained under British protection. It was administered by a resident commissioner, but tribal rule and customary law were retained except when they were repugnant to British conceptions of justice.

Swaziland became independent in 1968. Like Lesotho, it is a constitutional monarchy. The constitution provides for an assembly of which 24 members are elected by universal suffrage and 6 appointed by the king to represent special interests; the senate consists of 12 members, 6 nominated by the king and 6 chosen by the assembly. Swaziland has a population of less than half a million, of whom 8,000 are whites and own half the land. (This is unlike Lesotho where whites may, under permit, occupy land but may not own it.) Except for heat and malaria in the lowveld districts it is a healthy and fertile land. Swaziland has more hopeful economic prospects than Lesotho; and unlike Lesotho, which is entirely surrounded by the RSA, Swaziland has rail access to Lourenço Marques, which makes her less dependent on South Africa.

Botswana is by far the largest of the three ex-High Commission Territories but a great deal of it is desert or semi-desert scrub. She has a population of just over half a million and a fair proportion of adult men work on the Rand mines. Botswana is a republic, having become independent in 1966, and has a parliamentary-type president, a national assembly, and a house of chiefs. Unlike Lesotho and Swaziland, whose African population consists of a single nation, Botswana has eight major tribes of which both the best known and the most numerous is the Bamangwato.

Both historically and in their present-day relationship in southern Africa the three ex-High Commission Territories have much in common. All have a well-founded tradition of having been protected by Britain against absorption by the Transvaal and Free State and, later, by the Union of South Africa. It will be recalled that Selborne mentioned the possibility of the three territories uniting with South Africa, though he did not devote much space to the matter in his Memorandum. At the National Convention and in the South Africa Act the high priority was union of the whites, and the territories were relegated to a schedule of the Act which laid down the general rules to be observed if ever transfer of the territories to South Africa became a live issue. These terms included consultation of the wishes of the inhabitants, for even in 1909 informed opinion in Britain baulked at handing over, without their consent, the administration of these predominantly African territories to white South Africans who were just then drawing up a constitution that, in effect, entrenched white political power. As the twentieth century wore on it became increasingly improbable that any British Government would be allowed by public opinion to hand control over African territories to a white South African Government. South African governments, of whichever party, realized this and no formal approaches to the British Government were made; to have done so would have been to invite an outright rebuff which no South African Government would have cared to risk.

It was therefore left to individual prime ministers and ministers of foreign affairs to raise the matter with their opposite numbers in London. Smuts did so after the First World War and was turned down. Hertzog raised the matter with J. H. Thomas in 1935, at the very time that South Africa's race policies were hardening. Just before the Second World War Britain agreed to the setting up of consultative machinery between the Union and the territories, but by the time the war was over there had been little consultation, and the new Nationalist government in 1948 became more insistent in its demands that the territories should be transferred to South Africa. Malan, Strydom, and Louw—for many years minister of foreign affairs—all had a hand in trying to persuade successive British Governments that they were needlessly afraid of apartheid. By 1959 Verwoerd realized that it was a hopeless task and, as a practical statesman, abandoned it; but he publicly suggested that if the territories were being groomed for independence South Africa would willingly lend a hand in the matter of training personnel—an area in which, whatever may be thought to the contrary, she had considerable experience.

Despite increasing resistance on the part of Britain to South African requests it remained an open question whether the territories would not eventually be incorporated in South Africa. This uncertainty hampered effective development because successive British Governments, somewhat naturally, were not anxious to spend a great deal of money on developing an estate for South Africa to inherit. It bedevilled thinking in South Africa, too, to such an extent that the Tomlinson Commission[1] actually included the High Commission Territories in their maps and in their calculation of the amount of land that might be considered available for Africans.

It was not only because all three territories were ruled by Britain and desired by South Africa that they may be said to have had much in common. The very fact of being ruled by Britain gave them a certain cohesion, and a tradition of co-operation grew up in such matters as agricultural investigation and services, primary and secondary education, and a joint university at Roma in Lesotho. Moreover, geographic contiguity with South Africa gave them common experience of another kind. Lesotho is entirely surrounded by South Africa; Swaziland is enclosed by South Africa on all but one small sector; and the greater part of Botswana's boundaries, east, west, and south, march with territory controlled by the South African Government. In all three cases they are economically dependent on South African enterprise and on her railways and harbours. South Africa is their principal market for labour and produce and they, in turn, are a market for South African goods or for imports through South African ports. Customs dues on goods

---

[1] This Commission for the Socio-Economic Development of the Bantu Areas within the Union of South Africa was appointed in 1951 under the chairmanship of Professor F. R. Tomlinson. An official summary was published in 1955.

going in to the territories are collected by the South African Government and a percentage is paid over to the governments of the three countries. South African banks, insurance companies, building societies, and other capital enterprises operate in all three territories and South African rands and cents are their official coinage.

South African barristers and attorneys practise before the courts in all three countries and the common experience in law goes further than that. For many years the three territories have drawn most of their judges from South Africa, and the practice continues. The employment of South Africans, white and black, in other departments of government was common practice, though it has declined of recent years. Nevertheless, South African officials on loan to Lesotho are to be found in Maseru; African doctors and lawyers, trained in South African institutions, are to be found in all three territories. Indeed, it would not be too much to say that the administration of these territories would break down were it not for South Africans or for South African trained personnel.

This relationship between South Africa and her neighbouring territories is not confined to Lesotho, Swaziland, and Botswana. It extends, to a lesser degree, to Zambia and Malawi and to an even more marked degree to Rhodesia. Mixing in legal, educational, administrative, medical, and other professional circles in these countries, one is soon aware of the part played by South African institutions of higher learning in training personnel for southern Africa. For many years these institutions were the only ones that existed in southern Africa and they welcomed students from outside South Africa's borders. The strict application of apartheid in South Africa as well as the development of their own institutions in the newly independent countries has lessened the flow. But it has not dried up altogether, and the strong tradition, created over generations, persists. Such factors do not, of course, demonstrate the need or otherwise for a closer association between these countries and the RSA. But should such association become desirable on other grounds they would greatly facilitate negotiations.

Many features distinguish South-West Africa, in its relationship to the RSA, from the three countries just discussed. It is larger than the three of them combined and has an estimated population of about 600,000 or one-third their combined populations, and a higher proportion of its population is white—roughly one in six, as against Swaziland's one in fifty. Lesotho and Swaziland, and only to a lesser extent Botswana, became British territories as the result of white colonization, starting from the Cape and moving slowly inland, and the subsequent struggle for supremacy between Boers and British. It was not essentially part of the scramble for Africa. South-West Africa was. German settlement, under charter from the Imperial government, began in 1883 as a self-conscious and belated effort on the part of Germany to become a colonial power. A German protectorate was proclaimed over the enormous area as it is today and German authority in that area was recognized by the European powers. This did not mean that Germany had any hope or desire to populate the land but merely that it was thenceforth regarded as falling within the German sphere of influence. To a limited extent, however, the Germans did colonize. They built harbours at Luderitz and Swakopmund, set up a capital at Windhoek, and constructed a few hundred miles of railway. In the usual way of colonization, 'treaties' were made with African chiefs who had no authority to make them, and these were followed by revolt when the Africans realized that they had given away their land. Revolt was followed by 'pacification', neither more nor less brutal than elsewhere in the world where Europe was subduing non-Europe. It was the Herero tribe that suffered most in the pacification.

When the First World War began in 1914 South Africa, by agreement with Britain, invaded and conquered German South-West Africa, as the territory was then called. There was clearly no intention of returning it to Germany if the allies won the war, and in 1919 it was allotted to the Union of South Africa as a C Mandate, which entitled South Africa to administer it as an integral part of the Union. White South Africans began to buy farms in South-West and by 1925 the South African Government instituted a partially elected legislative assembly for which whites only had the vote. A long list of subjects such as Native affairs, mines, justice, posts and telegraphs, railways and harbours, defence, customs, currency and banking, were reserved for the Union parliament. The terms of the Mandate provided that the mandatory should 'promote to the utmost the material and moral well-being and social progress of the inhabitants of the territory'; but, judging by the annual reports of the Mandates Commission, South Africa failed to comply with this provision.

Before the Second World War there was some agitation for the return of South-West Africa to Germany; but the issue was never in serious doubt. Neither South African nor British Governments would have been willing to see Hitler's Germany control such useful bases. Moreover, South Africa had by this time a considerable emotional and economic vested interest in her 'ownership' of the territory. After the Second World War there was an increasing demand in South Africa for the full incorporation of South-West Africa. The matter was discussed at San Francisco (where the UN was founded) in 1945, and a year later Smuts raised it before the Trusteeship Committee, but by then the climate in which African territories and their inhabitants could be handed over to white control had long ceased to exist. Indeed, the tide was running strongly in the other direction—the direction by which African territories became independent of white control. The demand thus arose in international circles for South Africa to submit the territory to international control under a trusteeship agreement, which is what Britain had done in the case of Tanganyika, Germany's former colony in East Africa. This South Africa refused to do and so began the long and as yet unsettled dispute between the Government of South Africa and the rest of the world as represented by overwhelming majorities in the UN Assembly and the Security Council.

In 1949 the South African parliament passed an act which has been regarded by many as virtually incorporating the territory and making it a fifth province of South Africa. This is not strictly correct. South-West Africa was then given six seats in the South African House of Assembly and four in the Senate. Thenceforth she participated in South African general elections as she did in the referendum that approved of the republic. Moreover, the territory is as closely integrated in the economy of the RSA as are the four provinces. Nevertheless, there are three things that distinguish South-West Africa from, say, the Cape Province or the Transvaal. In the first place she is, by agreement, not subject to taxation by the South African parliament. Secondly, the white people of South-West Africa are by history, by tradition, and perhaps because of the great size of their country, less emotionally attached to the RSA than the people of the Transvaal or Cape Province. A high proportion of the white population is German speaking, and German habits and traditions have influenced the outlook of the whole area, white, black, and Coloured. It is doubtful if the Germans would want the territory to go to Germany; and few whites would agree to accepting decrees from the UN But the majority of whites have an independent South-

West African outlook that distinguishes it from the four South African provinces.

A third distinguishing feature is that, however much the South African Government may disregard UN resolutions, and however remote she may regard the danger of physical intervention to 'free' Namibia, she is tied by the fact that her rule in South-West Africa is not internationally recognized. No one doubts the right of the South African parliament to make laws for South African citizens in the Transvaal or Natal. But the nations of the world are practically unanimous in denying South Africa's right to legislate for South-West Africa. There have been numerous attempts by well-wishing nations to have the relationship between South Africa and South-West Africa settled by conference; but South Africa has refused to confer if her legal right to administer the territory were placed in doubt. When Liberia and Ethiopia, two of the original members of the League of Nations, instituted an action against South Africa before the International Court of Justice, in 1960, the Court found, after six years, that they had no *locus standi* except as parties to a dispute and could not institute action in regard to the mandate. This question-begging judgement solved nothing. The South African Government stood firm on its old ground in admitting that South-West Africa had indeed a special status but denying that South Africa was responsible to the UN for it. As long as the question remains unresolved, South-West Africa can be considered as neither independent nor fully incorporated into the RSA.[1]

The relationship between the RSA and South-West Africa is thus peculiar. South African laws apply to the territory—and this includes the numerous apartheid laws to which the rest of the world objects. The two major South African political parties (for whites only) are reproduced in South-West Africa; non-white political organizations that oppose white rule are to a large extent suppressed both in the RSA and in South-West Africa, but such evidence as exists indicates that they are strongly African nationalist. The same Christian churches that function in South Africa are found in South-West

[1] In January 1971 the International Court of Justice convened, at the request of the Security Council of the UN, to give an advisory opinion on the legal implications for member states of the continued presence of the RSA in Namibia. The stoyr of South Africa's conditional offer to the Court to hold a plebiscite on whether the inhabitants of Namibia wished to be governed by the RSA or by the UN, is well known and need not be repeated here. The offer added nothing to the settlement of South-West Africa's status and the position remains as it was.

Africa. With the differences already noted, South-West Africa is to all intents and purposes a fifth province of the RSA. Economically, she is not so much dominated by the RSA as integrated with it. She does not have a separate flag and her citizens do not have separate passports; she is not represented abroad except as part of South Africa. Yet there remains a doubt about her status.

The position of the three independent states of Lesotho, Botswana, and Swaziland *vis-à-vis* South Africa is clear. They are to a greater or lesser extent economically dominated by the overwhelmingly stronger RSA; and, in so far as economic domination spells political control, they are—to put it at its lowest—within South Africa's political orbit. Nevertheless, they are sovereign independent states with their own flags and anthems and citizenship, represented abroad by their own envoys enjoying diplomatic status. If a wanted man from, say, the Transvaal flees to South-West Africa he can there be apprehended by the South African police and brought back for trial to the Transvaal. If he escaped across the border to Swaziland and the South African police followed to arrest him, it would be a breach of international law which, unless settled, might have serious repercussions. In the first case South Africa would have considerable, though not unanimous support for doing what she considered to be within her legal right. In the second, she would have no support for violating the territory of a sovereign state. There have, indeed, been several instances where the South African police, in hot pursuit, have crossed the border of each of the three states; but the South African Government was quick to put the matter right. There are political refugees in all three territories, to the number of several hundred, and the South African Government has no legal means of arresting them. None of the three governments is likely to agree to an extradition treaty that applied to political refugees.

The relationship between these states and South Africa was perhaps most clearly set out for Botswana by Sir Seretse Khama in a statement before the UN General Assembly on 24 September 1969. He said:

Botswana is almost entirely encircled by minority-ruled territories. We have a long and indefensible border with Rhodesia, and a long border with Namibia and with South Africa itself. The only railway running between Rhodesia and South Africa passes through Botswana. Not only is this railway operated by Rhodesian Railways, but it is vital to both Rhodesian and South African interests. It is also vital to Botswana because it provides our only outlet to the sea and to export markets overseas. Through this route must come the capital goods necessary for our development. Unlike some other states in Southern and Central Africa we have no practical alternative outlet.

We are for historical reasons part of a customs area dominated by the industrial might of the Republic of South Africa. We share the monetary system of South Africa. Our trade and transport systems are inextricably interlocked with those of South Africa.

Sir Seretse went on to say that Botswana was compelled by economic need to allow some of her young men to seek employment in the mines in South Africa and that in the immediately foreseeable future there was little prospect of changing this. Botswana was making valiant efforts to cope with her economic and social problems, and the recent discovery of mineral resources would be of great help. Nevertheless, Botswana depended on foreign aid for more than half her revenue. She would welcome aid from any source whatsoever provided there were no political strings attached. 'We did not win our independence from the British to lose it to a new form of colonialism from any source whatsoever.'

Sir Seretse also said that Botswana recognized that she was part of southern Africa and that 'the harsh facts of history and geography cannot be obliterated overnight'. Botswana had noted South Africa's assurances of friendly intentions and her offer to assist, and though Botswana made no secret of her detestation of apartheid, he felt confident that she could coexist with the RSA without the sacrifice of national interests or fundamental principles. He said that

for obvious reasons Botswana must maintain diplomatic contact with South Africa. For equally obvious reasons we decline to consider an exchange of diplomatic representation until South Africa can fully guarantee that Botswana's representatives will in *all* respects, at *all* times and in *all* places be treated in the same way as diplomats from other countries.

At the conclusion of his statement Sir Seretse referred to what he called a more general point that also related to southern Africa. He looked forward to the development of a balanced and prosperous economy and a healthy non-racial democracy, not only for the sake of the Tswana but because it would permit them to 'make a great contribution to solving the problem of our region'. There was no question that Botswana would depart from the principle of non-interference in the affairs of neighbouring sovereign states.

But Botswana as a thriving majority-ruled state on the borders of South Africa and Namibia will present an effective and serious challenge to the credibility of South Africa's racial policies and in particular its policy of developing the so-called Bantu homelands and its stated goal of eventual independence for these Bantustans. It could force them to abandon the policy or attempt to make it a more immediate reality and even face the prospect of surrendering sovereignty to genuinely independent sovereign states. A prosperous non-racial democracy in Botswana immediately adjacent to South Africa and Namibia will add to the problems South Africa is already facing in reconciling its internal racial policies with its desire for economic growth.

For Botswana to sustain such a role it was essential that its independence be preserved and that it be 'insulated from any instability which the policies of neighbouring white-ruled countries may provoke'.

This statement by the President of Botswana has been dealt with at some length because what he said can, with variations, be applied to Swaziland and Lesotho. Swaziland, too, is almost entirely bordered by minority-ruled territories; Lesotho is entirely so bordered. Swaziland is the most prosperous of the three states and more than half her export trade is not with South Africa; she is therefore slightly more independent economically than Botswana or Lesotho. But she, too, depends on a customs agreement with South Africa and on the export of labour to the RSA. The leaders of all three are fully aware, whether comfortably or uncomfortably, of the need to recognize themselves as part of southern Africa. From all three countries there have been statements of a desire to live peaceably with South Africa while continuing to reject apartheid. All three are prepared to seek an exchange of diplomatic representation on condition that their envoys would enjoy full diplomatic privileges and immunity.[1] From her side, the South African Government has issued an open invitation to seek South African aid and to enter into trade agreements. There can be little doubt that the RSA, too, feels the need to live peaceably with her neighbours and is prepared to modify her policies—in regard to diplomatic privileges for non-whites —towards this end. When it is borne in mind that the three African states are all members of the Organization of African Unity, of the Commonwealth, and of the UN, it will be realized that they, too, have had to modify their international policies in regard to South

[1] Such an exchange already exists between South Africa and Malawi and there is a trade treaty between the two countries.

Africa. They cannot afford the luxury of whole-hearted and un-conditional condemnation of their powerful neighbour.

Perhaps the most important single link between all four states is the customs agreement. This was first entered into in 1910 when South Africa had just achieved union but was not yet recognized as a fully independent state,[1] and Lesotho, Swaziland, and Botswana were still the High Commission Territories with little vestige of self-government. Sixty years later a revised agreement was negotiated and signed between four independent sovereign states. It revised the method of calculating and dividing customs, excise, and sales duties in a way more equitable to the three African states and it virtually turned the territory of the four states into a free-trade area while allowing Lesotho, Botswana, and Swaziland to have protective tariffs on specified local industries. It regulated the marketing of agricultural produce and, finally, it established a Customs Union Commission as a piece of inter-governmental machinery for con-sultation to ensure the smooth running of the agreement and about matters of mutual interest that might arise.

At an official luncheon, given by the South African Minister of Economic Affairs to mark the signing of the agreement, sentiments of goodwill were expressed on all sides. Among other speeches was one by Mr. Peete, Minister of Finance from Lesotho, who said: 'Let us go on as we have begun, talking to each other, not at each other so as to ensure, in accordance with the letter and the spirit of this agreement, the continued economic development of the customs union area as a whole.'

Despite the considerable common ground that exists between South Africa and the three independent states of Lesotho, Botswana, and Swaziland, there are differences that must be examined. The first of these is historical and geographical. South Africa is today ruled by whites and, within the white *laager*, by Afrikaner National-ists whom most Africans regard as the lineal descendants of the Boers. As Africans see the history of the last 150 years, the whites have during that time occupied the whole of present-day South Africa over most of which their African ancestors had exercised rights of occupation as tribal law would have defined it. This the whites did, sometimes by force, sometimes by fraud, and frequently by a false theory that African chiefs 'owned' the land on which their

---

[1] We now know that, in effect, she was independent. But in 1910 dominion status had not been invented.

tribes lived and were able to dispose of it by treaty—that the chiefs were able to alienate tribal land.

In this conquest of South Africa the Boers played a significant part. In one way or another the Boers got possession of most of Natal, of Swaziland, of Tswana land on the Transvaal side of the Limpopo River and of tribal lands in the north-eastern Transvaal, of much land across the Caledon River from Lesotho that is today owned by Free State farmers and is still known as the Conquered Territory. In due course the Boers were conquered by the British and then formed a union. Within that union a predominantly Afrikaner nationalist political party came to power in 1948 and, at the time of writing in 1970, shows little sign of losing it. It was this white government that had at various times tried to persuade the British Government to transfer the protectorates to South Africa. To many Tswana, Swazi, and Sotho, therefore, South Africa is governed by the descendants of the Boers who had 'stolen' much of their land and would, if allowed, complete the process of alienation.

The boundaries of the existing states of southern Africa are artificial, and the reasons for the existence of those boundaries illustrate the historical differences between the states. To the Sotho, the Tswana, and the Swazi it was the Boers who had conquered them and from whom they had sought refuge in British protection. When the Lesotho Prime Minister once spoke about recovering Sotho land, it was from the Boers that it would have to be recovered; and the land in the western Transvaal that many Tswana still regard as theirs would have to be recovered from the Boers. To the Boers, however, Britain was the historic enemy. It was to escape from British rule that their ancestors had trekked away from the Cape. When they had established a republic in Natal, the British annexed it. After fifty years of independence in the Free State and Transvaal, the British conquered the Boers and annexed their republics; and during that fifty-year period the British had prevented the Boers from what they regarded as legitimate expansion of their rule over Africans by taking the Africans under their protective wing.

This greatly over-simplified account of the history of southern Africa cannot, of course, be taken as anything but that. It has been given here because it seems in these matters important to know what people believe the facts to be. For the purpose of reconciling two opposing viewpoints it is necessary to know not only what the actual facts are but also what the supposed facts are on which the two opponents base their respective views. African suspicions and fear of 'the Boers' may not, in the opinion of some, stand up to historical examination, but they may well be a potent influence on present-day attitudes. The man-in-the-street in Maseru or Gaberones may know nothing more about history than that his great-grandfathers fought in wars against the Boers. But that is enough to colour his views about the present South African Government. Indeed, the less he knows about history above that simple fact the more likely is he to distrust the descendants of the Boers.

Such feelings, rooted in history, have been fed by South African race policies. Those policies are avowedly based on the belief that the whites must continue to control the government of South Africa and that, to achieve that end, non-whites must be barred from any political influence that matters. Since the non-whites outnumber the whites by about 6 to 1, this must clearly mean that the whites are determined to maintain a minority government in perpetuity. Indeed, the very fact of being outnumbered is a reason for white determination to retain control. In the three African states under discussion, however, there is majority rule, and this distinction between them and the RSA constitutes one of the major differences that will have to be overcome if a federal association is to come about. This will be discussed later.

Another difference between the four states that acts as a source of friction is the refugee problem to which Sir Seretse Khama referred in the statement quoted above. This too springs from South Africa's race policies. Since there are discriminatory laws, there are people who will seek to alter them, and an ever-increasing spate of repressive laws is required to prevent this. The more it is forbidden the greater will be the volume of prohibiting legislation against which those who seek change will stumble. Minatory laws have never yet completely subdued determined men and women, and South Africa is no exception; as a result, a number of South Africans, of all colours, have fallen foul of the police on political grounds. Those who were caught and proved guilty were gaoled, but a number escaped across the borders into Lesotho, Swaziland, or Botswana.

Connected with the political refugee problem is that of South Africa's defence against attack from outside. Here, again, South Africa's defence problems are different from those of her neighbours. One of the threats to her security is the modern method of infiltration by guerrilla fighters whose object is to seek internal support for overthrowing the government; and the government naturally suspects that political refugees are among the infiltrators. Details of such operations are, for obvious security reasons, not made public. But it is well known that South African police are helping to repel infiltration on the border between Rhodesia and Zambia and that strict military watch is maintained on all South African borders. It has been suggested, too, that South Africa has an understanding with the Portuguese Government which is trying to suppress rebellions in Angola and Moçambique. As long as political refugees find safety in neighbouring countries, the whites in South Africa will fear for their security. In this respect South Africa's defence problem differs from that of her neighbours who obviously do not expect infiltration for the purpose of 'liberating' the inhabitants.

From a broader point of view, too, the RSA differs from her neighbours though, ultimately, their interests are the same. Being landlocked, they do not have to worry about seaward defence. This is South Africa's problem. The only defence problem Lesotho and Swaziland might have would be the defence of their borders against South Africa. It is highly improbable that South Africa would ever think it worthwhile conquering these two countries, but there is little they could do to prevent it. Botswana is in much the same position but she has a long common frontier with Rhodesia. There, too, the probabilities of a military clash are hardly worth discussing. Defence of southern Africa is, thus, almost entirely a problem for the RSA and it is only on her land frontiers that she and her neighbours have common ground, either for clashing or for co-operation. Even in regard to her coastlines, for which she alone is responsible, South Africa and her neighbours have much in common: it is their common means of access to world trade, and if South Africa were to be conquered the three territories could not avoid the same fate.

A further distinction must be made between Lesotho and Swaziland, on the one hand, and Botswana on the other. Botswana has a long common boundary with Rhodesia and her other northern neighbour is Zambia. She would like to increase her trade with Zambia and it was proposed, in 1970, to build a metalled road through Botswana to a ferry in the Caprivi Strip, which is administered by the RSA as part of South-West Africa, in the hope that this would enable her to increase trade with Zambia at the expense of the minority-ruled Rhodesia. There was an immediate unofficial protest from South Africa whose government is exceptionally

sensitive to any road-making in Botswana that might have strategic
value for South Africa's potential enemies. From the point of view
of defence, Botswana is of greater significance to the RSA than
Lesotho or Swaziland. The government of Botswana has been
scrupulous not to allow its territory to be used as a base for guerrillas attempting to infiltrate South Africa, but to South African eyes
the threat comes from beyond Botswana's borders.

There is one further difference between South Africa and her
three neighbours. She relies for fully half her industrial and mining
workers on sources of supply outside her borders—Malawi, Lourenço
Marques, and so on. From the three African states we are discussing
she gets about 180,000 workers a year. Now this might seem to be
a point of great mutual interest and benefit: South Africa needs
labour and the three territories need the revenue that comes from it
in the shape of remittances and taxes. In this common interest,
however, there lurks a serious cause of friction. At present, for instance, Lesotho has a surplus of labour because she cannot provide
employment for it, but it is conceivable that if her economy begins
to develop along industrial lines she will need all the manpower she
can get. This would bring about a serious conflict of interests which
could be resolved only if the two countries, Lesotho and the RSA
were part of the same economic and political complex.

5

CHANGES SINCE 1910

IN 1910 the southern Africa we are considering consisted of one Commonwealth dominion, three British dependencies, and one German colony. It was generally assumed that the three dependencies would eventually be incorporated into the Union of South Africa, and it is improbable that anyone at that time thought that South-West Africa would ever be anything but a German colony. Since 1910 the political picture has changed. The dominion left the Commonwealth and became a republic; the three dependencies became independent states and remained in the Commonwealth; the colony, having ceased by conquest to be German, has not yet attained a status that is internationally recognized.

These political changes are the outward manifestation of still more profound stirrings. Two world wars and industrial and technological revolutions so altered the political as well as the economic structure of Africa that we speak of the times before and after as colonial and post-colonial eras. Southern Africa did not escape the tide of nationalism that engulfed Africa. Indeed, South Africa herself was in the van of the nationalist movement. As early as 1912 both white and black nationalism had emerged in South Africa as the Nationalist Party and the African National Congress respectively, and the two movements were slowly maturing, on separate lines, long before African nationalism was born elsewhere in Africa. White nationalism had triumphed in South Africa by 1910, and the dominant group within the white group, the Afrikaner nationalists, achieved partial power before the Second World War and full power immediately after it. The African nationalist movement clashed with the whites, and when it began to assume threatening proportions after the Second World War it was curbed and eventually suppressed and driven underground. So the balance of political forces in the RSA has been upset and will seemingly remain in uneasy oscillation.

In southern Africa, too, as distinct from South Africa, the balance of forces has been disturbed. Lesotho, Botswana, and Swaziland have emerged in the post-colonial era as independent states, members of the Commonwealth and the UN. Before the 1960s South Africa dealt with the High Commission Territories through the British High Commissioner in South Africa; after 1961 the RSA dealt with the British Ambassador; and after 1966 and 1967 Britain ceased to be an intermediary and the RSA dealt direct with the three African states. It must be emphasized that, so far from isolating the three states, independence has given them the extra strength that comes from membership of the Commonwealth and the UN. Both these bodies now have an additional stake in southern Africa, and the RSA has to bear this fact in mind. Further north, too, all African states have become independent except Rhodesia, whose status is still undetermined, and the two Portuguese territories where the government is finding it hard to suppress African nationalist rebellions. South-West Africa, like Rhodesia, has an as yet un-determined status, and this very fact causes an imbalance in southern African politics.

Most of the newly independent African states openly dislike South Africa's race policy and sympathize with the suppressed African movements. As we have seen, there are strong economic reasons why South Africa's immediate neighbours and Malawi do not join in the hue and cry against her; nor, for political as well as economic reasons, does Portugal. In their dislike of the RSA's race policies the African states have found both the Commonwealth and UN effective international platforms to attack apartheid, and in the post-colonial era these attacks have found sympathetic international audiences. The world will tolerate, or at least not be noticeably active in suppressing, the sale of drugs, the growth of armaments, even slavery. But what it will no longer accept is discrimination on grounds of race or colour.

This changed international outlook, coinciding with the emer-gence on the African political scene of a number of independent states, has had a profound effect on the RSA's political thinking. While it may appear on the surface that it has merely hardened white attitudes on race, it has in reality either modified them or, at least, compelled white South Africans to reconsider their position. It has encouraged the RSA to seek friends among those black African states with whom she has some economic influence. It has had a restraining effect on her attitude to South-West Africa, for had it not been for the new trend in world opinion, she would long since have incorporated that territory. Most important of all, it has inexorably driven her into the logical conclusion of apartheid—the setting up of Bantustans with a promise of independence. Those who enjoy the power and privilege of minority rule may scoff uneasily at the inadequacies of majority rule in the new African states; but majority rule is a slogan no one can afford to deny or ignore. The white minority in South Africa is no exception to this.

In what used to be the Union of South Africa there are already two Bantustans in operation, with their own flags and national anthems and clearly demarcated boundaries; and six or seven more such regimes are in active preparation. Whatever may be thought about the limited powers entrusted by the South African Government to the Transkei, its existence and the prospect of further Bantustans are among the facts that make the real political map of southern Africa different from what it was in 1910. As Sir Seretse Khama said, in a statement quoted in a previous chapter, the existence of 'a thriving majority-ruled state on the borders of South Africa will present an effective and serious challenge to the credibility of South Africa's racial policies and in particular its policy of developing the Bantu homelands'.

As great, but more spectacular than the political growth, has been the economic growth of southern Africa since 1910, and more particularly of South Africa. This has brought into the open problems and dangers that were hardly apparent in 1910. In the first place, the Witwatersrand mining and industrial complex has come to dominate not only the economy of the Transvaal but that of the rest of southern Africa; and this economic concentration has become increasingly dependent on three resources which the Witwatersrand lacks—water, power, and labour. The supply of unskilled and semi-skilled labour is a problem that has hitherto been solved by migrant labour from the RSA's neighbouring territories. More than half the Africans employed in mining and industry come from outside South Africa's borders and there will be increasing pressure on her to improve the conditions under which migrants work. But apart from that there seems to be no obvious reason why the labour supply problems of South Africa will not continue to be solved in this way.

The supply of water and power is, however, not so obvious. It has become evident within the last decade that the economic growth

of South Africa will be stunted unless the supply of water and power
to her industrial areas can be much more than doubled. Since those
areas do not own the water resources for their needs they will
become, as in the matter of labour, increasingly dependent on the
countries that do—Moçambique, Angola, and Lesotho.

The second problem that has been uncovered by the economic
development since 1910 is the inefficiency of the historic provincial
boundaries which, it will be remembered, Steyn feared would be
perpetuated by federation. The comparatively small percentage of
the area of South Africa on which industries are concentrated is
densely populated and wealthy while the peripheries languish. It
is at least possible that the division of South Africa into natural
regions (about which there should be no need to be dogmatic or
rigid at the moment) would provide for a more even economic
development. There are parts of the eastern, midland, and north-
western Cape Province that, it seems probable, would benefit
economically if they were administered as separate units and not
from Cape Town. Similarly, there are areas of the western Transvaal
and southern Free State that would clearly benefit by a rational
system of local autonomy which, it must be pointed out at once, is
by no means inconsistent with central planning.

It is not only the international political climate that has radically
altered to produce a post-colonial era. The opinion is growing that
there is economic as well as political danger in the tendency for rich
states to grow richer and poor states, by comparison, poorer.
Economists have pointed out that it is the rich states that are best
able to avert this danger. That is the basis of aid to developing
countries, and the fact that such aid has been less than adequate
may be put down not only to the reluctance of rich states to part with
wealth but the futility of doing so without the most careful economic
and political planning.

In terms of the RSA alone such planning would probably involve
the partition of South Africa into natural regions, quite apart from
whether they would become autonomous. But the theory of assisting
developing areas applies outside the RSA's borders as well as
within. South Africa is not without experience in this matter. A small
percentage of her budget is earmarked for aid to neighbouring states;
she has lent both money and expert services to all of them, and her
own incipient Bantustans draw more heavily on her budget than
do the foreign states. If prevailing thought on international economic

arrangements is any guide, South Africa will be called upon to play an increasing part in the development of Botswana, Lesotho, Swaziland, and Namibia. This will be in her own interest quite as much as in theirs, and it will be irrespective of whether they join in a federation.

Another matter in which the southern Africa of 1970 differs from that of 1910 is defence. The South African Defence Force, established when she became a Union in 1910, was not called into action until 1913 when it and the Active Citizen Force were mobilized because of a national strike. In August 1914 the last Imperial troops were withdrawn and Botha's government undertook to capture South-West Africa, which constituted a threat to south Atlantic shipping, and to raise volunteer forces for service elsewhere. These decisions evoked a rebellion, chiefly in the Free State and Transvaal, in which personnel of the Defence Force itself became involved. When the government had suppressed the rebellion and taken South-West Africa, South African troops were sent to German East Africa and eventually to the Middle East and Europe, although there were not enough troops to form a division and they were brigaded with British regiments. Many South Africans distinguished themselves in the Royal Air Force and it was only after the war that a South African Air Force was established. During that war and the next, as we shall see presently, the naval defence of South Africa's coasts was Britain's responsibility.

In 1922 the Defence Force was once more called upon to deal with a general strike—the so-called Rand Revolution—and a rebellion, that of the Bondelzwarts, a Hottentot tribe in South-West Africa. During the 1939–45 war South Africa was much more deeply involved than previously. She helped to drive the Italians out of Abyssinia and had two divisions in the Middle East and, subsequently, one in Italy; her Air Force squadrons operated independently of the RAF; and, once more, thousands of South Africans fought in British regiments or in the RAF. She had coastal defence vessels and artillery, and reconnaissance aeroplanes, and her minesweepers operated in the Mediterranean. But, as in 1914–18, the main burden and responsibility of keeping the Cape route open for allied shipping fell on Britain. Since the war the Defence Force has been called out only once, in 1960, when, after Sharpeville, the government believed there would be an African uprising. Apart from the two wars, therefore, the Defence Force has been used only for internal security.

During two world wars South Africa's land frontiers were really in Europe and the Middle East and the defence of her coastline was almost entirely the responsibility of her allies. Her international status depended on whether her allies or her enemies won the war; and the victor in both wars was certain to be the side that controlled the Cape route between East and West. It is here that the possession of the naval base at Simonstown becomes important. This dockyard was a British possession until 1955, when she handed it over to South Africa in terms of the Simonstown Agreement, which gave Britain continued use of its facilities, particularly in wartime. Whether or not Britain has failed, as the South African Government has alleged, to fulfil her side of the bargain in the matter of supplying armaments, is not really pertinent to the question of Simonstown's importance in time of war.

There is a good deal of confused thinking in South Africa and elsewhere on this subject. In the first place, there is apt to be confusion in the public mind between Simonstown, a naval dockyard, and the harbour of Cape Town, a commercial port. When the Suez Canal was blocked there was a great increase of shipping via Cape Town. But this enhanced importance had nothing to do with war. It was a peacetime commercial activity, extremely profitable to South Africa and extended to ships of all nations. During a war enemy ships could only enter Cape Town harbour as captives or because their navy had cleared the seas of their own enemy. Simonstown, on the other hand, is important in war because it is equipped to repair and refit fighting vessels.

A realistic assessment of South Africa's naval strength, even potential, would show that she could never expect to defend Simonstown alone, except in the very unlikely event of her being attacked by a naval force as small as her own. It is in a world war that she becomes of importance, and she could not by herself prevent Simonstown from being captured by a much superior fleet. Ever since the Napoleonic Wars neutrality has been out of the question for South Africa. She must therefore choose her allies—those whom it is in her interest to see victorious, and who will be capable of helping her to defend herself against attack from the sea. In the present line-up of world politics it is highly improbable that South Africa will not be on the side of Britain and the United States, and she will not be allowed either by those countries or their enemies to be neutral. The mere possession of Simonstown does not, as is often thought, enhance South Africa's value to competing great powers.

This situation has to some extent been modified by Britain's withdrawal from many of her commitments in the Indian Ocean. South African ministers are apt to say that since Britain has 'run away' the defence of the Cape route depends entirely on the RSA. But this argument does not stand up to examination. For 'Great Britain' one might have to read 'the United States of America', but South Africa would still depend on a great power to protect the Cape route and would have to abandon neutrality and choose sides in a world war, the only kind of war in which the Cape route would be in danger.

Superficially it may seem as if South Africa's defence problems have not altered much since 1910. Her ability to ward off invasion by sea must still depend largely, if not to the same extent, on the naval strengths of the great powers; and her Defence Force will still have as one of its main tasks her internal security. Nevertheless, the problems have changed, subtly but fundamentally, since she became a republic in 1961. Until then she and all her bordering countries, with the exception of Angola and Moçambique were closely associated with Britain and the Commonwealth. When Lesotho, Botswana, Swaziland, Malawi, Zambia, and Rhodesia became independent they remained members of the Commonwealth, while South Africa withdrew from it. When the Central African Federation broke up, and subsequently when Rhodesia declared her independence, she and the Republic were doubly the two odd men out in the whole of southern Africa: both were minority-ruled states and neither was a member of the Commonwealth. Until 1961, then, South Africa had in effect no common frontiers with 'foreign' nations except Angola and Moçambique. All the others were members of a Commonwealth closely associated with Great Britain. Today the Republic has frontiers with seven foreign states of which four are members of the Commonwealth. This is a new fact to which those who are concerned with the problems of her defence are bound to give serious consideration.

South Africa's frontiers are no longer in Europe, nor is her landward defence any longer solely one of internal security. Before the Second World War and the succeeding wars in the East it would have been possible to argue that South Africa was in no danger from beyond her frontiers, for there were not then a number of hostile states in central, east, and west Africa. But even if this had been the case they would not have been able to attack so strong a country over thousands of miles of African terrain. The logistics of such an enterprise ruled it out of court.

Both these conditions have changed. Many African states are indeed hostile to South Africa, and modern methods of warfare no longer take much heed of distance. Guerrilla warfare has undergone revolutionary changes, and so have the effective weapons it makes use of. The changed tactics of infiltration have compelled defence chiefs in southern Africa to use new techniques. Army manœuvres in South Africa are realistically based on the threat of infiltration by guerrillas, and knowing that the success of such tactics must depend on the attitude of the inhabitants of the country attacked, army chiefs have been at some pains to associate African chiefs with their defence manœuvres. Furthermore, South African para-military forces are co-operating in Rhodesia against infiltration from Zambia and Tanzania.

If determined groups of South African citizens of the RSA were to welcome invaders in large-scale infiltration, a war of liberation might easily be sparked off. If, in addition, the RSA's neighbours were to sympathize openly or covertly with the invaders, she would be in grave danger and it is by no means certain whether, if left to herself, she would be able to control such a situation. But it is very unlikely that she would be left to herself to entrench white rule in southern Africa by force of arms. No serious thinking can leave out of account the possibility that the Security Council would be compelled to intervene in what would have become both a civil and a race war, a war, moreover, in which three Commonwealth countries would almost certainly become involved and in which, through South-West Africa, the UN would consider itself to have a major responsibility.

This change in her problems of defence has been brought about by post-war nationalism and decolonization, together with her own race policies. In the past South Africa's armed forces were called upon to maintain internal security; but except for the relatively minor South-West African campaign of 1914, they defended their country thousands of miles from her frontiers, in North Africa and Europe. There was never any direct threat to her borders. Today she has to guard her frontiers against the real threat of large-scale infiltration and possible revolt. Moreover, she has two formidable handicaps with which to contend: a security problem that in a war would be much more serious than in the past, and the fact that to a large part of the population of the world her enemies would be regarded as freedom fighters and she would forfeit the strength that comes from a belief in a just cause.

That, then, is the kind of war that South African governments must bear in mind. But they will still have to accept the possibility of a Third World War in which South Africa would inevitably be involved if for no other reason than that she lies on the Cape sea route and cannot remain neutral. In such circumstances she would, presumably, be able to contribute substantially to her own defence and that of her allies by her economic wealth and her manpower, and by her land, air, and sea forces. But her value as an ally is likely to be scrutinized in other terms—in terms, that is, of her relations with her non-white subjects, her Bantustans, and her immediate neighbours. If these relations are such that the RSA's armed forces are likely to be tied down to the defence of her borders and to internal security, her value as a potential ally will be considerably diminished. Furthermore, in the task that such a war would confront her with she would not be able to look to her allies for new weapons or replacement of old. She would, in fact, become an embarrassment to them. In this way her race policies have profoundly affected the problem of her defence.

To sum up, there are great differences between the southern Africa of 1910 and that of 1970. Then there were four British colonies, three British dependencies, and one German colony. Seven of these territories are today sovereign independent states and within one of them, the RSA, there are several potential sovereign states. In 1910 nationalism was only incipient; today it is triumphant or sufficiently threatening to be suppressed. And nationalism is a condition not readily accommodated within the constitutional confines of a unitary system. The rapid development of economic resources, the need to organize in an orderly fashion the transition from gold-mining to industry, and the knowledge that continued economic expansion depends increasingly on much greater supplies of water, power, transport, and labour, have altered the balance of economic forces. It has become clear beyond doubt that both continued prosperity and racial peace call for joint planning between the states of southern Africa. Finally, the growth of nationalism in Africa and the heightened awareness and detestation throughout the world of discrimination between people on grounds of race or colour, have altered the whole nature of defence problems in southern Africa. Considered in the light of existing political and constitutional arrangements, these problems are daunting and fall mainly on the shoulders of the RSA. And all these considerations seem to constitute a prima-facie case for reassessing the political structure of southern Africa.

6

THE CASE FOR FEDERATION:
NON-WHITES IN SOUTH AFRICA

To say that there is a prima-facie case for reconsidering the political structure of southern Africa does not necessarily mean that it should be reconstituted as a federation. It might become a union, though considering all the political and economic facts, that seems improbable. At the other extreme it might be a loose confederation—an agreement by treaty between sovereign independent states to act together in certain circumstances and on certain defined matters. Or it might be a *Zollverein*—a customs union—based on existing customs and other agreements between the autonomous states.

Applying the usual criteria—economic, climatic, geographic, social, and political—the form of political reconstruction that would have the best prospects of practical success seems to be federation. It is this form rather than the alternatives mentioned above that will accordingly be considered here, and a few preliminary (and cautionary) remarks are necessary before the difficulties in the way of it are analysed.

It is implicit in what has been said in previous chapters, but should here be explicitly stated and emphasized, that what is being considered is not a federation of five regions—the republics of South Africa and Botswana, the kingdoms of Swaziland and Lesotho, and the territory called Namibia. What we are considering is the federation of some fifteen regions covering the area of these five territories. What this implies will become clearer presently. All that need be said at this stage is that in the case of the RSA this would involve a double operation: redrawing the internal boundaries and altering the political structure of the RSA itself, and then federating with other independent regions. The first operation is itself a double one that must be carried out as one: this is the process of partition and federation which, for convenience, is referred to as partition/federation. The second one will be to federate the new federation with the other territories. This could—but need not be—carried out simultaneously with the first.

The second preliminary warning arises from the fact that people, faced with proposals for political reconstruction, too often assume that these will come into force immediately. They then put forward their genuine fears and decide, probably on insufficient evidence, that the difficulties are insuperable and that the disadvantages far outweigh the advantages. There are two comments to be made on this. Firstly, difficulties that appear insuperable in 1970 may wear a different aspect five or ten years later. For instance, the economic imbalance between the strongest and the weakest of a number of states may be so great as to make federation inadvisable. Yet this difference may be greatly reduced if not wiped out by the discovery of oil or by some revolutionary invention. In the same way, of course, the imbalance may be further increased. It is therefore well to be reminded that, as in all human enterprise, every care should be taken to examine all the ascertainable facts and to appraise the future in the light of these, avoiding on the one hand the optimism that believes that a scientific miracle will make federation possible, and on the other the pessimism that predicts unseen and unforeseeable difficulties. The real difficulties in the way of federation are neither increased nor decreased, though they may be concealed, by false analysis.

The second comment concerns the time factor. No one can doubt that serious attempts to cope with conditions in southern Africa must not be unduly delayed, but it is necessary to retain a sense of perspective. About a hundred years of social, political, and economic development preceded the federation of Canada in 1867. The thirteen North American colonies that won their independence from Britain in 1783 formed a federal union within a comparatively brief space of time; but it had taken a long and bitter war—a notorious foreshortener of time—to convince Virginians, Marylanders, Pennsylvanians and all the other people who today call themselves American citizens, of the desirability of federation. Even then it required a bitter and exhausting civil war eighty years later to drive home the lesson. In southern Africa there were abortive attempts at union or federation eighty years before the four British colonies united in 1910, and that was sixty years ago. What this points to is that, while southern Africa has reached the stage where delay in reconsidering her constitutional arrangements may lead to increasing crises, such consideration will take time to mature.

There is a third cautionary point to be made. It is fairly easy to assess the physical factors involved in federation. For instance, geographical and climatic conditions change slowly though they can to some extent be controlled by man. Economic conditions too are partly controllable and are certainly measurable. Such things as population growth, imports and exports, and national production may all be projected with reasonable accuracy, though, as we have noted, new inventions and discoveries upset the most careful calculations. Where, however, the factors involved are the results of cultural history and are embedded in such matters as social habit, racial and religious differences, or language, they are neither easy to measure nor to assess. In such cases the danger is not that they will be overlooked or ignored, but that they will be distorted and exaggerated and given values which, if history is any guide, they do not possess. For ways of life and habits of thought do undoubtedly change, and the extent to which such change can be revolutionary was experienced by the world in the second half of the twentieth century. It is, therefore, unwise to accept or reject federation solely on the grounds that habits of thought in such matters as race, religion, or nationality are immutable.

It is worth repeating these three warnings. We must not think of federation as between the RSA and four weaker neighbours, but as between a partitioned and federated RSA and four other areas. In the second place, it is necessary to retain our sense of perspective in the matter of time; and, thirdly, we must not be deluded into thinking that cultural habits of thought, however strong and apparently ingrained, are necessarily unchangeable. With these three precautions we may proceed to examine the factors involved in federation, and it is reasonable to start with the RSA as the strongest of the territories concerned.

A remark often heard in South Africa, particularly in the Cape Province and Natal, is that a mistake was made in 1910—there should have been federation rather than union. There is substance in that contention. In the first place, the weaknesses of the anachronistic historical boundaries, which Steyn saw, have become more apparent than they were in 1910. Since sovereign power is concentrated in a single parliament and executive, the political power that controls them has naturally tended to centre in the strongest economic province which is also the most populous in terms of white voters. Provincial powers to tax, to borrow, and to make ordinances are subject to control by the central government, and if it is under great pressure from the strongest economic province—in this case the Transvaal—it follows that the remaining three provinces will, from time to time, find themselves prevented from carrying out policies of which the central government may disapprove. This is particularly noticeable in primary and secondary education where pressure from the centre has forced Natal and the Cape Province to adopt policies and methods of whose excellence they were far from convinced. It is also true of such matters as race relations where the Cape Province has found itself compelled to enforce measures against Coloured, Asian, and African citizens which it would not have done but for great pressure from the Transvaal, supported in the main by the Free State, on the central government. It is precisely in these spheres that many Natal and Cape men foresaw the dangers and weaknesses of union. The 'ideal of uniform Native policy' so eloquently expressed in the years before union would seem to hold more dangerous weaknesses than are to be found in divergent policies.

One of the expressed objectives of the American Founding Fathers was to protect citizens against tyranny from within and without the USA. Perhaps one of the most striking weaknesses of a unitary constitution such as that of South Africa is its inability to protect individual and civil liberty against attack from within. This liberty is always at the mercy of the government of the day, restrained only by its good sense. When, as in the case of the Cape Coloured franchise, common sense conflicts with party interests, it is the latter that are likely to prevail. Moreover, a flexible unitary constitution is easily used by a party in power to forward its own interests at the expense of common sense and of the national interest alike. And however impartial the judiciary in a union may be, it has no constitutional authority to check the acts of a sovereign parliament. In a federal constitution the Supreme Court performs that function and prevents parliament from destroying individual or group liberty and from breaching the constitution.

Whether the common Native policy so strongly advocated in 1908 has been in the interest of non-whites is a matter of grave doubt. But whichever way one argues about apartheid, it represents that common policy. The logic of it dictates that there shall eventually be a number of separate Bantustans, of which the Transkei and Zululand are the first; and separateness involves the redrawing of the internal boundaries of South Africa, because the existing ones are no longer in accord with reality, at any rate with reality as implied in the policy of Bantustans.

In considering the possibilities of federation for southern Africa, there is one overwhelming argument for regarding the existing unitary structure of the RSA as a bar to progress. South Africa as a single unit is so strong in comparison with the other regions that they would, naturally, object to entering into a federation with her. No matter what safeguards were written into the constitution they would fear being ruled, in effect, by a centralized power, as the present provinces of South Africa are. If South Africa retained her unitary constitution her race problems would not only, as now, dominate the provinces, but would almost certainly spread. As we saw earlier, federation is not advisable where there is too great a difference in economic strength among the federating units. It is true that such economic imbalance could be altered by new discoveries, but the facts as we see them today would militate against the success of a federation in which the RSA was one unit. This situation would be changed if the RSA herself became a federation of some eleven autonomous regions, no one of which would appear so disproportionately powerful to Lesotho or Swaziland or Botswana as the RSA does now.

There is another reason why federation in the RSA is a precondition of federation in southern Africa. If the RSA retained her present unitary constitution, great world pressure would be brought to bear to prevent federation, pressure on Lesotho, Botswana, and Swaziland to reject all overtures for federation as a trap to entangle them in apartheid laws, and even greater pressure on South Africa to prevent her from incorporating, as it would appear, Namibia as a fifth province. Whatever happens, suspicions and fears of the RSA's race policies will not easily be dissipated in the African states and the world. These fears will be dealt with later. Here it is sufficient to say that they may be reduced if South Africa should alter her constitution as part of a wider scheme of federation, and that without such alteration federation of southern Africa is not likely to come about.

Only a few of the major weaknesses and disadvantages of South Africa's present constitutional position have been mentioned here, and others have been referred to in other parts of this book, where its retarding effects on economic development were discussed. In general it would seem that a case could be made out for the partition/federation of the RSA into a number of autonomous regions on the grounds of administrative convenience and efficiency, of a sounder power-political structure, of safeguarding individual rights and liberties, of encouraging cultural diversity, of sound economic development and as a precondition of a wider federation. There are, of course, many difficulties to overcome, some of which will be discussed presently. But the main difficulty will be to persuade the white voters of the RSA to unscramble the constitution—to redraw the internal boundaries and reconstruct the constitution on federal lines. So great is this difficulty that no one would be bold enough to suggest such a constitutional upheaval merely for the sake of what many might regard as minor administrative and economic advantages.

For South Africa to change to the kind of federation contemplated here would involve drawing a new map in which the present four provinces are replaced by, say, eleven regions, which might include four Bantustans with adjusted boundaries. This is a political operation not essentially different from delimiting parliamentary constituencies, and could be performed by a judicial commission whose terms of reference would permit it to take into account such factors as natural resources, size of population, cultural and historical affinities. Though any suggestion must be rejected that the object of the operation is to separate the races, there is no reason why racial composition of regions should not be a factor, particularly where, as in the case of tribal areas, that is already an existing fact. Theoretically, federation would consist of eleven South African autonomous regions, and a federation between these and Lesotho, Botswana, Swaziland, and Namibia would then follow. In practice, however, there is no reason why the final stages should not be reached concurrently, so that at a given time all fifteen states would enter into federation.

The major political difficulty, as with all federations, would be to decide on what matters the regions, and on what the central government, would have sovereign legislative powers. In the case of South Africa alone there is much experience to guide us, and the legislative powers of existing provincial councils should at least form a basis for deciding on the sovereign powers of the autonomous regional parliaments. Such matters as defence, banking and currency, posts and telegraphs, and harbours seem to be more suitably controlled by a central authority. South Africa is not a highly centralized country, and an operation to centralize further might be complicated, but not fundamentally difficult to arrange in the light of her experience. The question of fiscal arrangements—of deciding on the respective taxing powers and revenue of centre and regions—is bound to be a difficult one, and it would be closely related to existing economic resources. There would, no doubt, be tough bargaining about this between the prospective regions, but there is every reason to believe that the problem is susceptible of practical solution.

These are two of the major problems of partition/federation in the RSA. Others will become apparent. It was pointed out, however, that for the twenty million South Africans the federation we are discussing has a twofold aspect. Provided they can be persuaded of its benefits, the partition/federation of South Africa does not present insuperable difficulties. The second stage or aspect, that of joining with other regions that are at present foreign independent states, presents more. To this we must now turn, and after a brief discussion of the way in which such great issues are likely to be judged by the population at large, consider how federation with other states might appear to South Africans.

Although they may have a final vote on the acceptance or rejection of a proposal, few individuals consider national issues in isolation. Democratic consultation normally takes some such course as the following: an issue comes before the public through their political leaders, through press comment, and through radio and television. There is much casual and informal discussion and argument between individuals, based on information arrived at in this way, and against a background of personal hopes and fears. How will the decision affect me personally? Will I be better or worse off? Since many of the factors are complex and not readily grasped by people unaccustomed to dealing with such matters, political leadership will obviously play a dominant part in helping individuals to make up their minds. This normally operates through organized parties, and if there is more than one party, the pros and cons of any national issue stand a good chance of being thoroughly ventilated.

In South Africa this form of democratic consultation cannot take place on a country-wide basis because no machinery exists for consulting all adults as one voting unit. Nevertheless, machinery does exist for consulting what might be called the constituent elements of the population. Assuming that two-fifths of the population is adult, a breakdown would give approximately the following numbers of voters:

White: 1·5 million	Sotho: 0·6 million
Xhosa: 1·5 million	Shangaan: 0·7 million
Zulu: 1·6 million:	Venda: 0·1 million
Swazi: 0·2 million	Other African: 0·1 million[1]
Bapedi: 0·6 million	Coloured: 0·8 million
Ndebele: 0·1 million	Asians: 0·3 million
Tswana: 0·7 million	

In all these units, except the one called 'other Africans', machinery exists, and has been used, for popular elections; in most of them there are opposing parties and leaders. It is true that the individuals of the racial units are spread over wide areas, for they are not compact groups, but for the purpose of finding out their views on federation this would not be a difficulty. The members of the different groups would in all probability think of the question in terms of how it would affect their group, but one would hope, and could reasonably expect, that there would be leaders of sufficient stature in every group to consider the question of federation in its wider aspects as well as from a narrow nationalist point of view. It would be their task to lead their own people on what they believed to be the right road. If federation with neighbouring states is to be brought about, it is essential that it should have the approval of the majority of all South Africans. The machinery to ascertain this is already in existence.

It is impossible to say what considerations would move the Xhosa, Coloured, white and other electors if a proposal for such federation were finally put to them. But it requires no prophet to say what issues are likely to be uppermost in the minds of their leaders; and it would be those issues that would determine the voters' attitudes. We must once more remind ourselves, however, that the relative importance of issues does change. All we can do now is to talk about those issues that today seem to us to be most likely to be prominent and even crucial.

Coloured and Asian South Africans have no homelands in the sense that Zulu and Xhosa do, and the question of their ever being separate independent states does not arise in practical politics.

[1] This consists of smaller tribal groups that could be consulted separately.

Electoral machinery exists for ascertaining their views as separate groups, but there is reason to believe that if they were to vote on the question of federation, there would be little objection to their votes being counted by the electoral machinery that is used for white voters. Coloured and Asians regard their interests as being identical with those of the general population, and many white people agree with them. In such matters as the kind of federation here proposed, in defence or currency or banking, they would not regard themselves, as the Xhosa might, as having 'special' interests. What they will, of course, want to know is whether they would continue to be confined by law to certain residential areas, to certain jobs, to different rates of pay, to separate education and to separation in amenities such as public transport. These questions, as we shall see, are among those that will interest all South Africans.

It is possible that the proposed delimitation into autonomous regions might result in a region in which Coloured people are in a majority. If this were to happen it would, of course, be known before any voting took place and it might affect the attitude of Coloured voters. They might then think of themselves as a separate national group, as Zulu or Tswana might, whose regional problems differed from those of other regions.

The leaders of the four major African groups that have been envisaged as having a near-independent status by the time a federation might have to be decided on, would be exercised by problems that were apparently different from those of other regions, but they would be essentially the same. The emphasis might be different. What in one region would be a question of freedom to seek employment, could, in another, be a matter of supply of labour. Here are some of the questions that would naturally pose themselves to Xhosa leaders and followers if called upon to choose between a federation and a separate national existence; and for Xhosa read Zulu or Tswana or South African Sotho. Would they be able to come and go freely throughout the length and breadth of the new federation or would there be inter-regional restrictions on, for instance, the flow of labour? Would old labour laws remain in force or would Xhosa be allowed freedom to join trades unions anywhere in the federation, not only in their own region? Would wage rates and salaries everywhere be the same for all who were qualified for a particular job? Would the many colour-bar restrictions in force in South Africa today remain in force in the federation?

These questions and many more are of concern not only to Africans. Like those that seemed to have particular relevance to Coloured and Asians, they all concern everyone and cannot be answered in isolation. The answers to most of them are subject to two over-riding questions: what sort of a federation is proposed, and to what extent would relations between a regional government and the federal one be different from the existing relations between, say, the Transkei and the Government of the RSA?

The kind of federation proposed will obviously depend on whether the participating regions desire a closer or a looser form of federation. On very general lines it might be suggested that a looser form would best suit the wide geographical and cultural differences between different regions. In general terms, too, it might be that cultural interests should remain regional, and economic interests federal. Closer definition of such broad terms is full of pitfalls. There are always matters that should clearly be federalized, such as banking and currency, though regional powers are less easy to allocate. But there remain not only the so-called residuary powers but also the problems that might arise from, for instance, the control of water resources: it might seem natural today to suggest that the regions should have control over their own water resources, but in twenty years' time it might be destructive of the whole purpose of federation not to have federal control over the distribution of power that comes from water resources.

Whether the contemplated federation is close or loose, a division of sovereign powers between central and regional authorities cannot be avoided. Such powers will, of course, be co-ordinate, not sub-ordinate the one to the other. Leaving aside for the moment what this will mean at the regional level, at the federal level it can only mean a parliament, probably bi-cameral, in which the lower house represents the people of the federation and the upper house represents the regions. If the lower house represents the people it can only be on the basis of a common franchise; and in the upper house the regions will have equal representation. In the federal legislature, executive, and administration there can be no discrimination on grounds of colour or race.

There are powerful arguments against this aspect of federation and these will be examined when dealing with the reactions of the white rulers of South Africa to federation. For the moment we are concerned with the feelings of the people of those regions, such as the

Transkei or Tswanaland, that are predominantly African in racial composition. Those regions do, at the present time, actually have a franchise based on race, for no white or Coloured inhabitants of the Transkei may vote for the Transkei legislative assembly. It is improbable, however, that there would be any serious difficulty in such regions in the way of changing to a non-racial franchise.

The second overriding question concerns the relations between central and regional governments and this depends on the answer to the first. In a federation the regions will have sovereign powers exercised co-ordinately with those of the central authority. In those subjects allocated to them by the agreed federal constitution—the act of federation—regions could not be overruled by any superior sovereign authority for there would be no such thing. Nor, of course, could the regions make laws on subjects allotted to the central parliament. In case of dispute between the central and a regional authority, the Supreme Court would be called upon to interpret the constitution.

The relationship between a region and the centre would thus differ markedly from that between a present-day province or Bantustan and the Government of the RSA. Today, all regional legislation is subject to central veto; the subordinate legislation is subject to legislation by a sovereign parliament. Today, the South African parliament can alter the subordinate legislative power of provinces or Bantustans. Under a federal constitution that can be done only by constitutional amendment for which the procedure can be made extremely difficult and yet not impossible.

Under the existing South African constitution the legislature of one province cannot interfere in matters in which it is competent for another province to make ordinances. Only the central government can veto such ordinances. Similarly, in a federation the legislature of an autonomous region cannot interfere in matters on which another autonomous region is constitutionally competent to act. Neither can the central government. If it is thought that an act by a region is unconstitutional, the Supreme Court decides and its decision is final. But there is another way in which the autonomy of regions in a federation may be contrasted with the subordinate legislative powers of provinces. It was pointed out that, if there was a large majority of the supporters of the governing party in the central parliament, in an overwhelmingly strong province, their influence on the central government might be used to influence its attitudes towards provincial ordinances. In practice this has made it possible for a strong province to exercise undue influence on the kind of legislation that the weaker provinces may wish to make. This could not happen under a federation. Even if a very strong region wished to impose its will, via the central parliament, on weaker regions, the central government itself would be powerless to do so. This radically alters the relationship between regions and centre. Under the unitary system in South Africa today the provincial administration has, as it were, to go cap in hand to the sovereign central government. The citizen of an autonomous region in a federation would not feel that his welfare services depend entirely on what his administration can extract annually from a central government. Decisions that closely concern him and on which his region is competent to legislate under the constitution would no longer be taken by a government in which —on these particular matters—he is represented only through his own administration. To take a simple example: the voters in an existing province may find that an education ordinance, passed by their own provincial council, is vetoed or radically altered by the central government. That could not happen to a voter in an autonomous region in a federation unless the law in question conflicted with the constitution and was found by the Supreme Court to do so. These are some of the questions that present voters and those who would become voters under a federation would have to consider.

The extent to which the essential independence of the regions in a federation can be maintained must depend on whether they have adequate financial resources to operate in the fields of legislation and administration that have been allocated to them by the federal act. If, as at the moment in regard to the provinces, the right to tax and to raise public loans, as well as the amount of the grants-in-aid from the central treasury, all depend on the goodwill of the central government, to be sought afresh annually, talk of regional independence would be unreal. Rich and poor regions alike would have to be assured of enough income to meet their basic needs. This would have to come from a pool of revenue collected by the central authority but it would by no means be a grant as it is now. It would be revenue by right, not by favour, and the region would have the sovereign right to decide its own priorities of expenditure as, for instance, between education and roads. A difficulty about this system is that it may be inflexible, but there would seem to be no reason why there should not be a federal economic commission, equivalent in standing, say, to the supreme court, that could review quinquennially the amounts to be drawn by each region and by the central parliament. Such a body would not recommend to the central government, for that would once more make the amount depend on central goodwill. Once the commission had decided on the annual amount to be drawn by each region during the next five years that decision would become legally operative. A possible objection to this is that it removes a financial decision from a popularly elected body and places it in the hands of a commission. It is said that this is contrary to democratic practice, but in every country in the world, whatever its constitution, financial decisions of this nature are being made daily by ministers or by appointed committees. Moreover, once the revenue has been allocated its expenditure is subject to normal parliamentary controls.

A second source of regional revenue would be from direct and indirect taxation. In all federations this is a difficult matter to arrange equitably and there are no hard-and-fast guiding rules except that, as with the guaranteed revenue, once the bases of federal and regional taxation have been agreed upon by the act of federation, the right to tax is solely within the discretion of the central and regional authorities themselves. Because of the fluctuating nature of revenue and expenditure it might be advisable to have similar revisionary machinery as was suggested for the fixed revenue.

It is almost impossible to arrange fiscal matters so that regional and central authorities are financially independent of one another. It is still a sound principle of public finance that the authority that spends money should be responsible for raising it. But even the most careful arrangements could not avoid some system of grants by which less wealthy regions are able to carry out their functions. There would, therefore, have to be compromise, as there is in every country. The problem is to see how the compromise can do least harm to sound financial principles. It must be remembered that the relation between taxation and expenditure has been altered because the purpose of taxation is, today, not solely to collect revenue to cover public expenditure. More and more there is the additional purpose— to regulate the economy. There must be overall planning in a federation, and those who draw up the constitution will have to be careful not to hamstring the central authority's ability to regulate the economy of the whole country.

One of the greatest needs in a modern society is to assure people of their rights and liberties irrespective of skin colour or religion or sex. It is notoriously easy to talk eloquently about the absence of these in other countries while excusing it in your own. It is also notoriously difficult to secure these rights and liberties by laws, unless they carry the full support of the great majority of citizens in any particular area. There may be laws prohibiting racially segregated schools; but if thirty or forty per cent of the people in a racially mixed area are determined not to have integrated schools, such schools will only be established by methods that make a mockery of education. Most countries have had this problem for generations. That they have failed to find a perfect solution is no reason for not continuing the search. The independence of regional and central governments in a federation was discussed earlier. Clearly that independence of legislative authority cannot be allowed to be destructive of civil liberty. Lincoln said you cannot have slave and free states in the same union, and the USA has not yet fully recovered from the war between the states that wanted slavery and those that did not.

To minimize the danger of a modern society breaking up on this question of racial discrimination there is one way that offers hope: to embed a bill of rights in the constitution. This can only be done in a federal constitution which is safeguarded by an independent judiciary. That is, indeed, the paramount advantage today of a federal as against a unitary constitution. It must be repeated that rights and liberties cannot be guaranteed unless the citizens of a country want them to be. But it is at least possible to make it extremely difficult to breach those rights and liberties. In an area such as southern Africa a bill of rights that defines the rights and liberties that may not be infringed by legislation is essential. This may be regarded by some as a limitation of sovereignty. It is, rather, a deliberate self-denial of its own sovereignty in certain fields, by a sovereign act, in order to secure those values that are universally regarded as fundamental.

There are other matters on which the leaders and the people of the predominantly African regions, here called Bantustans, would want information to enable them to decide whether or not to enter into a federation. Two of these are a national anthem and a flag about which it is neither necessary nor particularly useful to say anything here. These are symbols and, as such, always likely to cause emotional explosions; but in none of the countries under consideration are they so deeply embedded as to constitute serious obstacles to compromise or change. The question of language is more important. The Bantu languages are reputedly rich in literary value and of the greatest psychological importance socially, but as far as can be judged now they would be of little use in a scientific and technologically dominated world. Citizens of small European countries have built up great literatures but found that if they wanted to enter into the world of international thought they had to do so through one or more of the so-called world languages. This would apply to all the inhabitants of southern Africa, and the world language most widely used here is English. It does not seem probable that those conditions will change in the near future, and for the time being at any rate practical considerations would require each region to have two official languages of which one would be English. Taking everything into account it would probably be wisest to have both English and Afrikaans as the official languages of the federation. It must be emphasized, however, that all such matters are not susceptible to theoretical solutions. The solution will emerge from arguments at the conference table by the people most concerned.[1]

Another question that will naturally arise concerns those African members of the four Bantustans we have been considering who are not permanently domiciled in their homeland. These may constitute as much as two-thirds of the total African population of the RSA. A Xhosa living permanently in Johannesburg or Durban votes in Transkei elections, but no method has yet been found by which he can be regarded as a Transkeian in practice as well as in theory. One possible answer to this problem is to increase the size of the homelands; if federation has become a practical policy this would not present any serious difficulty, but it is no real solution. Whatever the intention behind the creation of Bantustans was, it could not have been that they contain all Xhosa and all Zulu. Economists are unanimous in saying that this is not practicable. Even if the area of each homeland were to be doubled it would still not be economically possible in existing circumstances.

The conception of Bantustans as entirely 'black' states by the creation of which total separation between white and black may be achieved on a national scale, must be, and to a large extent has been, discarded. This does not, however, mean that if the map of the RSA were to be redrawn and existing Bantustans regarded as autonomous

---

[1] India faced similar problems but on a much larger scale, and solved them in some such way as is here suggested.

regions of a federation, with an entirely different political and economic status from that they now have, such Bantustans should not be predominantly African. In delimiting autonomous regions of a federation, racial composition might well be a factor, always provided that it is not the sole criterion.

The question remains: what is the future of those Africans who, for all practical purposes, no longer have a homeland? In existing circumstances there is machinery for them to take part in their Bantustan elections and they will presumably do so in any referendum about federation. But what are they—and for that matter, what is anyone interested in the future of southern Africa—to be offered as an inducement to vote for federation? There seems to be two alternatives. They can remain citizens of their own homeland, taking part in its regional elections and voting for its representatives to the federal parliament. They would be guaranteed certain rights and liberties at present lacking, such as the right to move freely and to form trade unions in defence of their conditions of service. They would still be migrants but their status would be more akin to that of Italian and Spanish migrant workers in France, Switzerland, and Germany—that is, they would have freedom of movement and would be protected by their own governments.

On the other hand, they could cease to be citizens of their own homeland and become citizens of the region in which they are permanently domiciled. A good deal would depend on how the regional boundaries work out in practice, but we may assume that in a region where there turns out to be a small majority of whites there will be strong opposition to any large-scale influx of African citizens. Something more will be said on this aspect in a subsequent chapter.

Allied to this question is another. There are more than one and a half million Africans who belong to smaller tribes than the large groups we have been considering. There are 568,000 Tonga, 395,000 Swazi, 346,000 Ndebele, 280,000 Venda. Between them they represent about half a million adults whose voice would have to be heard on any federal issue. Many of them live in tribal reserves and would be able to vote on federation in the same way that the Xhosa or Zulu do. But their position after that would be more precarious than that of Africans who belong, whether by domicile or by tribal affinity, to an acknowledged autonomous region. On present evidence their own homelands are too small and fragmented to be constituted as

Bantustans. That may presumably be corrected, but their numbers scarcely warrant it. A possible solution is to regard such reserves as regions not yet fully equipped to become independent members of the federation, much as Alaska was for many years, and give them an associate membership. Such federal associations are not unknown. Those Africans would then be no worse off than those who have a regional homeland but are domiciled elsewhere, and their citizenship status would be improved by being associated with the federation and under its constitutional protection. This is, however, one of the many problems that cannot be solved on paper and about which it is not at this stage possible to do more than suggest lines upon which a solution may be sought.

Assuming, as we must, the continuation of the Bantustan policy to its logical conclusion in independence, there would be many advantages to them in joining a federation such as is here proposed. Their economy would be immensely strengthened, their international status enhanced, and they have nothing to lose except an independence that, in isolation, might prove more apparent than real.

This chapter has been mainly concerned with the non-whites of the RSA and we must now turn to the Africans in the existing independent states and to the whites in South Africa.

7

THE CASE FOR FEDERATION: SOUTH AFRICA'S NEIGHBOURS

IN considering whether or not they want a federation such as is here envisaged, non-white South Africans have to ask themselves two questions: do we want a partition of the present RSA into, say, ten or eleven regions and, secondly, but simultaneously, do we want them regrouped as a federation? From what has been said so far there can be little doubt that such a federation would have much to offer the sixteen and a half million non-white citizens of South Africa. Citizens of Lesotho, Botswana, and Swaziland, for the most part non-white, have only one straightforward question to answer: do we want to join such a federation? For South-West Africans, white and non-white, the question is more complicated and will be considered separately.

Though there are local differences between Lesotho, Swaziland, and Botswana, and between their relations with the RSA, the general pattern is the same and they may be considered together. These three states will naturally be fearful of the disadvantages that might result from joining their powerful neighbour—a neighbour, more-over, whom they have previously had reason to fear and who is, today, unpopular in world opinion and, more particularly, among their own fellow African states. The first of these disadvantages would probably be the loss of an independent international status, a matter on which Sir Seretse Khama, in a speech previously quoted, spoke feelingly when he said how much Botswana prized her independent membership of the UN and the international platform it gave her.

Such international status is not only a matter of prestige. It carries with it a considerable measure of international protection against aggression or discriminatory action from outside; and it carries with it membership of UN agencies that, for a developing country, are invaluable. As members of a federation these states would not be able to take an independent line in foreign affairs; and it is at least conceivable that at some time in the future Botswana or Swaziland might find itself at loggerheads with other members of the proposed federation in its relations with its other neighbours. Botswana might wish to pursue a different policy towards Zambia from that adopted by the federation as a whole.

A second disadvantage would be loss of membership of the Commonwealth. It is difficult to assess this in concrete terms. The Commonwealth is not a cohesive body that takes strong political or economic action. It protects the interests of its smaller members, such as these three states are, but only in very general terms, and where the economic or military interests of the members diverge no common policy is possible.[1] Nevertheless, there are considerable advantages in belonging to the Commonwealth. Its collective influence is widespread and great, and there is much to be said for belonging to a 'club' where the rules, though flexible, on the whole make for a humane and non-racial outlook on life—an outlook that tolerates, and even welcomes, diversity. There are, moreover, fringe benefits in belonging to the Commonwealth—courses of Commonwealth studies in Britain, places at British universities, interchange of students and university staff, close links with a wider culture, freer access to all that is implied in the term Western civilization, and possibly the most important of all—participation in a remarkable system of communications that was developed while the Commonwealth was the British Empire. South Africa may be of greater immediate importance to the three states, but membership of the Commonwealth assures them of participation in the cultural life that lies beyond the limits of southern Africa. Moreover, in the conduct of foreign affairs, these smaller countries have the inestimable advantage, at no expense to themselves, of being represented by Britain in many countries to which they could not afford to send diplomatic representatives.

Lesotho, Botswana, and Swaziland might be fearful of losing these advantages if they joined in a southern African federation. They might also fear the loss, or the deterioration of their own culture and language. They might, in fact, see federation as an up-to-date imperialistic trick to ensure the continuance of white domination.

---

[1] This was written before the Conference of Commonwealth Prime Ministers in Singapore during January 1971, where there was indeed great divergence between the policy of Great Britain (in the matter of supplying arms to South Africa) and most other members of the Commonwealth. Nevertheless, the Commonwealth survived this formidable clash.

And the white domination in this case will not be the reasonably benevolent rule from distant London but that of upholders of apartheid as practised by South African whites. The feeling might be that, as things are now, the three states enjoy many of the advantages of having a strong neighbour without having to surrender their sovereign independence. Why change that happy state of affairs?

These legitimate fears would have to be set at rest before the leaders in the three states would or could persuade their followers to agree to federation. The way to do this is to meet the arguments honestly, if possible to counter them, and to provide a strong incentive by pointing to the positive advantages of federation.

The counter to the argument that joining a federation would mean the abandonment of national sovereignty and the consequent loss of international prestige is that, on the contrary, an isolated state with a small population is likely to increase, rather than diminish, its prestige by joining a large and prosperous federation. None of the advantages that are to be had by membership of the UN and UN agencies would be lost; and their immediate value might well be more direct in their impact because they would come through the superior organization and expertise of the large state. In this case, the federated regions of southern Africa would have at their disposal all the advantages of a strong existing organization and expertise in such matters as agricultural development, health services, and pest control, and the benefit of international association in addition.

Though there are limits to the contention that the largest political units are likely to be the most economic, small political units are no longer economically viable in the modern world. Nevertheless, the world will be the poorer culturally if small units are all to be amalgamated. Federation is a possible answer to the problem of how to achieve the advantages of economic size without sacrificing the cultural values of smaller units. The three states we are considering, and the Bantustans of South Africa, will remain economic and cultural backwaters if they cling to an independent status. By federating they could join in the prosperity of a large economic unit while retaining their cultural independence. A federation such as is here suggested would be able to deal realistically with such vital questions as the distribution of water and power, marketing, labour demand and supply, transport, and international trade agreements. No modern state can prosper without economic planning, and federating with South African regions would enable Lesotho, Botswana, and Swaziland to share in the efficient planning of the whole of southern Africa.

It was suggested earlier that the inhabitants of the three states might argue that there was no need to sacrifice their independence since they in any case enjoyed many of the benefits of association with their stronger neighbour. Commercial and fiscal arrangements already exist on a satisfactory basis; so, to a certain extent, does the availability of expert services. And even more of these benefits are to be had for the asking, because the RSA herself is anxious to share in the development of neighbouring states. This argument could well be put forward by political leaders who see their own personal prestige and authority being diminished if they enter federation. The answer to this argument is threefold: in economic matters, so-called independence is largely illusory. Secondly, Botswana, Lesotho, and Swaziland by no means share fully in the benefits of associating with a stronger economic unit. To take one example, their international trading relations and borrowing powers would be greatly strengthened by joining a federation. Thirdly, the existing commercial and fiscal benefits would be strengthened, not endangered, by being institutionalized.

The risk of losing the advantages of membership of the Commonwealth is more difficult to discount. Great Britain is in many ways the hub of the Commonwealth, and, both historically and by tradition, she has considerable interest in having racial peace in southern Africa. She also has heavy vested financial and trade interests in the RSA. Britain is therefore likely to take a sympathetic view of any scheme such as federation that held out clear promise of racial peace, and it is not beyond the bounds of possibility that the advantages of membership of the Commonwealth would not be wholly withdrawn from former members. Indeed, they have not been wholly withdrawn from the Republic of South Africa.

The fear, for which there is some historical justification, that federation may be a trick to spread apartheid is even harder to counter because, like that other fear that is partly responsible for apartheid itself, it has strong emotional roots in the subconscious, and rational arguments against it lose their sharpness and impact. If the people of Botswana, Swaziland, and Lesotho believe that all white men, and particularly white South Africans, are inherently hostile in their intentions and determined to maintain white domination in southern Africa at all costs, then it will be difficult to induce them to federate with the RSA.

It will be difficult, in any case, but not impossible. We do not have to assume an inherent hostility on the part of all whites to explain the present attitudes and policies of the RSA. The more probable explanations are, firstly, fear of losing the privileges that economic and political power bring, and, secondly, the determination of Afrikaner nationalists to preserve their language and their culture. Such rational explanations do not, however, cover all the facts. Strong subconscious and emotional feelings induce many whites to regard blacks with fear and hostility. Rational arguments and reasonable actions are not likely to demolish such fears, in either black or white, but they may at least lessen them and make way for a saner approach.

Fear of losing the privileges that accompany power is a common phenomenon. Nor is there anything unusual about the measures taken by those who wield power to retain it intact. Power and privilege should not be confused. When we speak about a class in society having political power we mean that all decision-making rests with that class or its agents—decisions about what shall be the law and how it will be carried out. The meaning of 'class' varies in time and place, having different connotations in, say, the eighteenth and nineteenth centuries, or in Germany and England. There have been class distinctions in most parts of the world for at least two thousand years and the ruling classes ruthlessly suppressed any attempt on the part of other classes to wrest power from them or even just to improve their lot, if that involved defying authority. Slave risings in Rome, and more than a thousand years later in America, peasant risings in England and Europe, and trade unions in the twentieth century, were all put down with a ferocity that indicates the lengths to which a ruling class will go in defence of its power to rule.

A ruling class is not an organization, though it may set up and support organizations to advance its interests by controlling the political machinery of state. The growth of the ruling classes in Britain and on the continent of Europe was a long, slow, and complicated process in which the Crown, the Church, and the nobility were all involved. It might take centuries for a class to achieve political power, but once that had happened the ruling class became exclusive and was loath to share its power by admitting other classes. No one not born into the ruling class could enter it except by a kind of tacit consent. There may be shifts of power within a ruling class itself and an ambitious individual or a group may seize power by force or fraud; but power still remains within the class which will not surrender it to other classes unless compelled to do so by force.

The connection between economic and political power may be obvious or subtle. It is often said that the 'great industrialists' are the real wielders of political power and that the politicians and statesmen are puppets. This is a half-truth. Industrialists are not a united body with a single policy; they are in competition with one another. They do, however, have a common interest in general economic matters, such as the supply of labour, markets, taxation, and fiscal policy. It is probably more true to say that there is a balance between economic and political power and that, so long as this is reasonably maintained, the 'great industrialists' will not be unduly concerned and will not seek to influence political decisions. Even then, it is political power that counts, and the wielders of economic power can secure their interests only by affecting political power.

A class that has achieved political power will not surrender it except as the result of revolution or conquest. But there are examples in history where a ruling class has agreed to share its power, either because of threats of revolution or when it believes it to be in its own best interests to do so, which is often the same thing. Examples of this are to be found in nineteenth-century Britain and Europe where the political franchise was extended to other classes by the ruling class. This was sometimes the result of revolution, but after 1830 the revolution was often not much more than a street demonstration. Another example is to be found in the way in which employers have yielded some of their economic power to their workers. When employers decide to recognize trade unions, and when enlightened employers associate workers with management, they are in fact admitting their workers to share in the control of industry which influences political decisions.

The white rulers of South Africa, like ruling classes everywhere, have entrenched themselves and may conceivably not surrender or even share power unless forced to do so by revolution. The race laws may have other objectives as well, but their main purpose is to entrench white political power and thus to preserve economic and social privilege. But while the whites will not surrender power except under *force majeure* it is not impossible that they may come to see the advantages of sharing power. There are already signs that those who wield economic power in the RSA are aware of the advantages. There are also signs that they and those who wield political power have become more acutely aware of the disadvantages of refusing to share power. These disadvantages were set out in Chapter 1: stagnation or violence. When the ruling class in South Africa comes to realize the real nature of its dilemma, it may find that sharing power may be much less difficult under a federal than under a unitary system.

The second motive of apartheid is the determination of Afrikaners to preserve their language and culture, which they believe to be threatened by alien cultures. It can be argued that a culture is not preserved by isolating it; it merely becomes fossilized. This happened in China and Japan until their isolation was destroyed. It may even be argued that the so-called cultural motive for apartheid is merely a rationalization to justify and cover up the economic motive, but this is too facile a view. There is nothing unnatural or unusual in the Afrikaners' determination, in the context of their history and political development, to preserve their way of life and to reach out for the political power which they believe will enable them to do so. The deplorable race laws have not come about because those in power deliberately willed evil for its own sake but because they were deluded into believing that their security and freedom lay in depriving others of theirs. Once this principle had been accepted and embodied in legislation, all the rest followed and ever more stringent laws became inevitable if Afrikaner nationalism was to remain in power.

If there is validity in these assumptions about the origins of apartheid, several conclusions are relevant about the fears of Lesotho, Botswana, and Swaziland that federation would mean the importation of apartheid into their countries. In the first place, white domination in South Africa, being fundamentally economic, depends on a large non-white working and consuming public. As a white witness before the Fagan Commission said: 'We need them and they need us.' There are many indications that the wielders of economic power in the RSA will take this into account in their thinking about South Africa's neighbours as well as about the RSA itself. As practical business men it is improbable that they would try to enforce so unpalatable a doctrine on states whose co-operation is essential to their economic enterprises. South Africa's trade and other relations with these three states have, since 1961 at any rate, tended to cut across strict apartheid rules. Cabinet Ministers from Malawi have been officially entertained in the most expensive 'white' hotels, and so have Ministers from the Transkei. The South African Prime Minister, Mr. B. J. Vorster, paid an official visit to Malawi in 1970 and other Ministers have visited a number of African states. There is no reason why this process, so far from ceasing at federation, should not be speeded up. Official visits give a kind of sanction to ordinary business exchanges that preceded them and have, in fact, been taking place for many years.

This does not imply that apartheid will vanish at the stroke of a federal pen or that the fears of South Africa's neighbours are groundless. Though they may have roots in the subconscious they are real enough, and apartheid in the RSA is a grim fact. But if it is based on economic facts it is neither inevitable nor immutable. It is unrealistic to believe that trends in Africa and the world will not make apartheid give way. There are already within the white ranks in southern Africa serious misgivings about the practicability, let alone the morality, of such race laws. Nevertheless, the people of the three states concerned will want more solid assurances than liberal hopes. These may be sought, firstly, in the fact that there can be no racial discrimination within a federal government. If Xhosa, Zulu, Tswana, Sotho, or Swazi help to elect a federal parliament, white South Africans could not, even if they wished to, impose apartheid on such a structure. This point, in so far as it concerns white objections to federation, will be elaborated in a later chapter. Here, we are concerned with the probable reactions of the African populations of the three neighbouring states. For them the argument is simple: a racially discriminatory federation is a contradiction in terms and not to be considered.

An assurance that this non-discriminatory structure would not be altered after it had been neatly tied up may be sought in the fact that there could be some seven predominantly non-white autonomous regions in the federation. The personal liberty of their citizens could not be curtailed by a federal parliament against the will of the regions. Their autonomy would be guaranteed in the federal constitution which could not be altered except by extremely difficult constitutional procedure, and it would be protected by an impartial judiciary. Moreover, a bill of rights would be written into that constitution and its provisions similarly protected. These are powerful bulwarks against domination by any one class or race.

The position of Namibia differs markedly from that of the three states we have been discussing. It was a German colony, while they were British colonies or protectorates. They are now independent sovereign states solely responsible for any decision about entering a federation; and neither in theory nor in practice is Namibia independent. Other individual states, or the Commonwealth, or the UN collectively may tender advice to the three states, but they would have no legal grounds for trying to prevent them from joining a federation or even for condemning them for doing so. In regard to Namibia, the UN Assembly formally revoked the mandate that South Africa had exercised, and in 1970 the Security Council, by 13 votes to none, with Britain and France abstaining, resolved to call on member states to issue a formal declaration that they considered the continued occupation of Namibia illegal. Moreover, in August 1970, the chief of the Herero said at the funeral of his predecessor that he would continue to call upon the UN to administer the territory until it was ready for independence. In these circumstances the majority of the states assembled at the UN would undoubtedly feel that they had a right to be consulted, and if they thought fit, to prohibit the RSA from including Namibia in a federation or in any other way altering her status.

In considering Namibia as a candidate for federation with southern Africa, the first thing, as in the case of South African non-whites and the three states adjoining the RSA, is to find out how the inhabitants of the territory might regard the matter; how they would think their interests affected. Two further points—to be considered in the next chapter—are the attitude of the present rulers of the RSA to federal proposals and the reactions of world opinion.

There are approximately 100,000 white, 30,000 Coloured, and 500,000 black inhabitants of South-West Africa, a total population of about 630,000 or about half that of Lesotho, twice that of Swaziland, and equal to Botswana's. The territory has, proportionately, many more whites than the three independent states. The Odendaal Commission found, in 1968, that there were twelve 'different and divergent' population groups and suggested that seven separate 'nations' should be recognized, the other groups being too small. The policy of the RSA Government is to recognize six 'nations' on the lines of Bantustans in the Republic, but one of these, the Herero, is only 24,000 strong and its members are scattered throughout the territory. It is, indeed, difficult to believe that these groups can be effectively reorganized except, possibly, for the quarter of a million Ovambo who live in an unfragmented area.

Much as one must regret the tribal wars and white colonization that played such havoc with African tribal life and, in this case, fragmented their traditional though undemarcated land and scattered the tribesmen, the important thing now is to ensure the well-being and contentment—freedom from want and freedom from fear—of the present groups. This will not be done by the artificial revival of small ethnic remnants, and these could not in any case form viable regions of a federation, though Ovamboland might just possibly prove an exception.

As we saw in this and previous chapters, it is a practical proposition to ask the inhabitants of the Transkei or Zululand, Botswana or Lesotho, whether they wish their territory to become an autonomous region in a southern African federation. These groups have well-developed and cohesive political machinery for ascertaining public opinion. Both the question and the method of getting an answer are straightforward. With the possible exception of the Ovambo and the Rehoboth Basters, the question would be meaningless in South-West Africa and the means of ascertaining the answer would be of doubtful effectiveness. There is little point in asking the scattered 24,000 Herero or the 60,000 Damara, of whom ninety per cent live outside Damaraland, whether they wished 'their country' to join a federation. They have no real country. The Rehoboth Basters have a well-established council dating back to German days, but their population is too small to be considered as an autonomous federal region.

It was suggested above that Ovamboland was a possible exception and that its people could reasonably be consulted. Their problem in arriving at a decision would be simpler than in the case of, say, Lesotho. They have no Commonwealth relationship to consider and they have no international status apart from their position as inhabitants of Namibia. As we have seen, that status is of little practical account. All their interests are linked with those of the RSA and it could only be to their advantage to have a more assured position within a federation.

Decisions of and about the non-whites of South-West Africa must to a large extent depend on what kind of federal association is envisaged. It is not the purpose of this book to provide a blueprint for southern African federation, but here as elsewhere some concrete suggestion may be a help to discussion. There are two possibilities: South-West Africa could become a single autonomous region or it might be partitioned into two such regions, the predominantly white south and the predominantly non-white north in which the Ovambo would be in the large majority. In either case the small non-viable groups would presumably have some form of local self-government, but theirs would not be autonomous regions.

While postponing discussion of UN approval of a federation which would include Namibia, let us assume that such approval has been sought and obtained. Given this, the non-white inhabitants of South-West Africa would have much to gain and little to lose by federation. They would continue to share in the economic prosperity of southern Africa; and they would no longer depend on the doubtful support of the UN for an illusory independence free from white domination. As members of either one or two autonomous regions they would participate in the elections of the federal government and would enjoy the protection of a bill of rights.

The white citizens of South-West Africa, too, would have much to gain from a federation. We saw earlier that there is a distinct South-West African outlook that regards white South-West Africans as different from—possibly more independent than—other white South Africans. It is not altogether certain that they would vote for complete union with the RSA, such as would be their lot if the territory were fully incorporated as a fifth province. It is almost certain, however, that they would vote for a union that did not mean unity. A federation in which their independent outlook would be allowed free play would suit them better than closer union. It would also suit them better than the present uncertain constitutional position. Their international status would no longer be in doubt and they would no longer have a 'special status', subject to continuous and heated international debate.

8

THE CASE FOR FEDERATION: WHITES IN SOUTH AFRICA

THE part of southern Africa we have now considered holds almost twenty-four million people. Of these, close on four million are white and their rule extends over some twenty million occupying over three-quarters of the area, and their economic control or influence dominates the whole of the area. Some of the advantages and disadvantages of federation, as it might affect the eighteen million non-whites in and out of the RSA, have been considered, and I have tried to estimate their reactions to proposals for federation. They constitute more than eighty per cent of the total population in these territories, but merely to count heads is to distort the picture, and discussion that minimized the importance of the four million whites would be unrealistic. It must be borne in mind, however, that the present imbalance of population will increase as time goes on. The *Statistical Yearbook* for 1966 shows that, by the year 2000, South Africa will have seven million whites and thirty-five million non-whites.

However meagre the prospects are that four million will be able to continue exercising political power over eighteen million—let alone seven million over thirty-five million—and however unhappy the consequences of failure to do so may be, we are dealing with the situation as it is now, in which power rests with the four million. If a majority of the white voters of the RSA wanted a federal arrangement with her neighbours, there would be no need for them to consult the Zulu or the Xhosa, though it would certainly be wise to do so. Similarly, if Lesotho, Botswana, and Swaziland all rejected the invitation to join a federation, that would not stop the white voters from partitioning the RSA and turning it into a federation. And if the majority rejected federation there would be no point in further discussion. This is not to say that, as in 1910, non-white opinion need not be consulted or that, as in the case of the Central African Federation, they should be consulted and their evident wishes ignored. Federation without honest consultation of all adults would be a farce.

But the economic and political strength of the four million whites in southern Africa is so overwhelmingly greater than that of the eighteen million non-whites, that their wishes, as distinct from their interests, are in fact paramount.

The argument in previous chapters has been that the present race policies of the white rulers are leading white and non-white alike into stagnation or racial conflict. It was further argued that a substantial minority of white voters know this to be the case, and a majority feel that there must be something wrong with policies that the rest of the world so heartily detests. A majority of white voters, therefore, would in all probability welcome a change, provided their present privileges are not reduced without compensating advantages; they might, indeed, be prepared to surrender the luxury of the universally unpopular white domination provided their interests, as they saw them, were safeguarded. In previous chapters, too, many facts were given with a minimum of comment. The time has come to consider the argument and the facts as they may influence the attitudes of the white voters of the RSA.

As little as we can assume that all non-whites, or even all Xhosa or all Zulu, hold the same views, so little can we take it for granted that all whites will hold the same opinions about, or react in the same way to, federation. People are individuals and it is as such that they are members of groups—by race, occupation, religion, politics, or social and cultural affinities, and they remain individuals however much they may be influenced by the beliefs prevalent in their group. It is not, therefore, very helpful to say that 'white reactions are likely to be', or 'white voters will feel'. Nevertheless, in order to be comprehensible and to give reasonable content to the discussion, I am compelled to divide people into categories, trying to limit the number of them but well knowing that the fewer there are the more we shall have to generalize.

Since the question the voters of the RSA will ultimately have to decide is that of federation, the main groups will be political parties to whose leading men and women the voters will look for guidance. Most people are in all probability not active members of a political party and their political activity is confined to voting at election time. It is to these people that the core of the political party must appeal if it wants to achieve office, which is the object of any political party. Those who control the party will therefore have to frame policies that it can persuade the electorate to accept. In arriving at its policies the leaders will be moved by their own vision of 'what the country needs' and by political pressures from organized groups of people who, by occupation and inclination, are able to lobby in protection of their supposed or real interests. In most groups these interests are mainly conceived of as economic, however much this may be disguised. Relevant to federation, such interest groups in South Africa might be composed of the following: farming, commerce, labour, mining and industry, and the professions generally. These are all well organized and capable of exerting pressure on political parties.

There is a division of opinion that cannot be ignored, that between those who favour and those who oppose racial separation. This division cuts across many others, but while it divides people politically and often in such social matters as religion, it is becoming less strong in questions that affect their economic interests. Moreover, many people who favour voluntary or customary racial separation do not believe in it as a national policy. On the whole, therefore, these cannot be classed as interest groups; but political leaders and parties will not be able to ignore this division. Their policy in regard to federation would be the outcome of their convictions and pressure from organized groups, but they would have ultimately to make that policy palatable to the voters and in presenting it to them to take into account more than the influence of interest pressure groups.

As with the voters of the Transkei or Zululand, white voters would have two questions to consider: whether they wanted the RSA to be partitioned and then federated and, if so, whether they wanted to invite other states to join the federation. These two questions cannot logically be considered separately because the decision on the first must influence that on the second. A vote for partition/federation might not necessarily mean a vote for wider federation, but a vote against it would mean exactly this, because federation between the RSA as a unit and her neighbouring states would be of the one-horse-one-rabbit variety and the smaller states are unlikely to accept the role of rabbit. It is reasonable, therefore, to consider the two questions as one while noting where they may properly be separated. In other words, in considering the reaction of white voters we are really considering the suggestion to partition the RSA, reunite it as a federation, and then to combine with other African states in a federation of southern Africa that would consist of some fifteen regions.

White voters in South Africa would ask themselves whether this is what they wanted, whether this is how they envisaged the future of their country; and they and their leaders would be likely to have in mind the following considerations, here grouped in order of convenience: division of powers between the federal and regional governments, together with administrative and financial arrangements; racial policies; defence.

The first of these questions was touched on in Chapter 6 and elsewhere and it is only necessary to repeat that this book does not pretend to be a blueprint for federation. Details of the division of powers between centre and region, finance, the administration of justice, and many other matters cannot be dictated beforehand but could only be decided at conferences of the statesmen who would be negotiating, advised by their experts. It is likely, moreover, that the final issue as presented to the electorate would be shorn of complicated and confusing details with which the voters were not particularly concerned. It is possible that a few matters such as control of broadcasting or higher education might arouse public controversy, but it is more likely that what the voters would want would be an uncomplicated picture of what such a federation meant. What this is has been made reasonably clear in this book without going into minuter details.

It is perhaps worth summing up and repeating what has already been said: instead of the present four independent states there would be some fifteen autonomous regions, and sovereign powers would be divided between them and the central legislature. The regions would naturally be different from the existing divisions, sometimes smaller, sometimes larger than now, but the exact boundaries are a matter for negotiation based on expert advice. In arriving at such boundaries, economic, cultural, ethnic, and historical considerations may all be given weight but none, particularly the ethnic, would be a sole reason for demarcating a particular boundary. Some of the autonomous states may well be the same as some of the present Bantustans, with adjusted boundaries. The legislature of the central government and those of the regional governments would be constitutionally assured of the basic income necessary to carry out their functions and this would not depend on the good graces of other regions or of the central government. There would be a bill of rights written into the constitution and, like the constitution, safeguarded by a federal supreme court. The constitution itself would not be alterable except by a procedure which would require something in the nature of a two-thirds majority in three-quarters of the regions.

These are some of the major differences between the proposed federation and the system of government to which white voters have been accustomed. What are the reactions likely to be of the categories into which I found it convenient to divide these voters? Agricultural services, loans, marketing of produce, and labour may be supposed to be of paramount importance to farmers. It is improbable that services and loans would be any less or any more efficiently organized under federation than at present. Smaller and more natural regions would possibly enable farmers to organize their activities more effectively than is possible in large unwieldy provinces with distant central control. The marketing of agricultural produce and the maintenance of a reasonable balance between agriculture and manufacturing prices constitute a world-wide problem. Price maintenance requires a central authority and there is no reason why this should not be possible under a federation. On the other hand, it may confidently be expected that the creation of an effective internal market for produce would be facilitated by federation.

It is in the matter of African labour that there would be a major difference. Africans who work as farm labourers and come from, let us say, the Transkei are today all migrants in the sense that they have no right to be anywhere except in the Transkei. When they sell their labour anywhere outside their homeland they do so by permit which can be revoked at any moment. In a federation they would be citizens of an autonomous region irrespective of whether they were domiciled in that region, and as such their right to move freely in search of work would be guaranteed by the constitution and enforceable anywhere in the federation. This, so far from being a disadvantage to agriculture, is something that economists and progressive farmers have long believed in. It would provide a stable and far more efficient labour force. Many South African farmers would, no doubt, see the matter in a different light, but it would be difficult to disprove the facts. It may be argued that a reform of this kind could be made under a unitary system. That is so, but it is notoriously difficult to get legislation to improve agricultural wages and terms of employment in a parliament dominated by landowners, such as England had in the early nineteenth century and South Africa has today. If a federation were to come about, this reform would be part of the general reshuffle.

Commercial, industrial, and mining enterprises in the RSA can hardly but welcome federation. Apart from access to raw materials and power, what they look for is an effective market and a good labour supply. It is becoming generally recognized that what South Africa needs to maintain an expanding economy is the development of internal markets. Industrialists and mining companies are as dependent on labour as is agriculture, and they have for long had efficient machinery for recruiting it from both in and out of the RSA. Though there is not a shortage of mine labour, industrial employers are today at a disadvantage similar to that which farmers experience: their labourers work for them on government permit and are essentially migrant. In a federation they would be free to seek work where they wanted to—that is, where the demand was greatest—and they would be able to organize, to improve and protect their terms of employment. Moreover, it is highly probable that the present labour structure, based on job reservation, would have to be considerably modified under federation. Most economists and a great many industrialists would agree that to free both employer and worker from their present shackles would contribute materially towards the creation of a more stable, a better paid, and a more progressive worker, and that this, in turn, would help to create a greater internal market.

The modification of job reservation might frighten white workers who are at present heavily protected by colour-bar legislation and custom against losing jobs to non-whites. A great many white workers, however, do not fear the additional competition that job reservation is supposed to avoid, and they have solid economic grounds for wanting the abolition of industrial colour bars. They as well as most employers would probably welcome federation if it necessitated the removal of employment restrictions based on race. This is true of white workers and employers irrespective of party-political affiliations. Indeed, the government itself in its capacity as a big employer of labour has been forced to modify its practice, though not its theory, in the interests of efficiency.

There is one further occupational category to consider, namely the professions. Professional men and women are likely to ask about such matters as the division of powers between the central and regional governments, how they affect their own personal position, and whether or not they will make for greater efficiency and higher standards in their particular profession. Medical doctors, for instance, will want to know how their salaries in government service and in hospitals would be affected and whether hospitals and other public health services would be more efficiently run under a federation. There is no answer to the first question and no simple answer to the second. Salaries will always depend more or less on the economic health of the country. As for the proficiency of professional services, general experience seems to favour central policy-making with a great deal of decentralized administration. This is possible in either a unitary or a federal system of government. Finally, for effective organization the professions require some form of national legislation regulating the terms on which new members are trained for and admitted to the profession and, thereafter, a code of professional ethics. If such legislation and regulation were regionalized it would inevitably result in differing standards and, possibly, in a lowering of standards. This is something the professions might fear while welcoming the administrative decentralization that federation could afford. There is, of course, no reason why such legislation should be regionalized.

In all these categories there would be 'those who favour and those who oppose race separation as a national policy'. This long label was deliberately chosen because others are apt to convey a false impression. To use the words Nationalist and non-Nationalist would be inaccurate since there are many non-Nationalists who favour racial separation, though perhaps not as an official policy; and there are Nationalists who do not favour it as a national policy. The words liberal, conservative, or even progressive are either meaningless within the existing framework of South African politics or have a distorted meaning. The division of white voters into those who favour and those who oppose race separation as a national policy is, moreover, particularly appropriate in the context of federation. Men and women in the other categories we listed may act in some sort of concert when considering how their group interests will be affected by the administrative and financial arrangements proposed. But their actions are less predictable when it comes to the question of racial policies that are likely to cut across other interests. It is to this question of racial policy—the second of the considerations I suggested would occupy the attention of white voters and their leaders—that I must now turn.

It would probably be true to say that, at present, a large majority of white voters favour some degree of social and political racial separation, but it is not a large majority that favours racial separation as an official policy, something done by act of parliament and enforced by the police. Many of those who want separation are prepared to accept voluntary segregation. It is in fact one small minority that believes so strongly in the necessity for separation that they are prepared to see it applied as a national policy no matter what the cost in economic prosperity, international disapproval, or even ultimate disaster. That the majority are not prepared to pay what they consider as too high a cost, is clear from the appeals made by their leaders that they should be ready to make sacrifices for apartheid. Most people would, of course, like to have their cake and eat it— to enjoy the personal privileges which apartheid seems to assure to the whites without paying the price, but a growing number of whites in South Africa regard apartheid as a policy that does great harm to human relations and damages the country's economy, and they are working for its ultimate abandonment.

The social, political, religious, economic, ethical, and humanitarian pros and cons of apartheid have been set out and argued in many books and publications, and this is not the place to add to the list. All that need be said here is that the majority of white people in South Africa are in a position of political and economic power and that they regard some form of separation as a safeguard of their culture, their privileged standard of living, and their political security, and they are not convinced by arguments that apartheid is no real safeguard. If the people who believe that it is a safeguard were asked to consider federation they would naturally want to know to what extent federation would mean giving up such a policy, what would replace apartheid as a protection of their privileges, and whether there were compensatory advantages in changing from their present policies.

Racial policies everywhere in the federation would of necessity differ from existing policies in the RSA. They would have to do so in all federal matters. There could be no first- and second-class regions, and citizens of autonomous regions would have to be assured that their rights were recognized everywhere in the federation. Positions in the federal civil service and in the federal parliament would be open to all citizens and it would be constitutionally impossible to apply such restrictions on movement as the present pass laws entail. Nor could there be restrictions based on race in any of the services provided by the federal government, such as transregional public transport or the post office. It is probable that in a predominantly white region there would be a strong urge to apply discrimination in purely regional matters. It is hard to see how this could be avoided, as experience in the USA has shown. A bill of rights cannot list any but general rights and liberties, and for a citizen of a region to obtain protection from what he might consider a discriminatory law, he would have to show that it destroyed one of the general rights or liberties of the people.

There is a difference between policy embodied in legislation, and custom that is strong but has no legal sanction. In the RSA such matters as admission to restaurants, places of entertainment, and even to beaches are all governed by laws that distinguish between a number of racial groups. The same is true of owning property or living in an urban area. This was not always so, particularly in the Cape Province where such matters were frequently a matter of custom. Laws that enforce segregation can clearly have no place in a federation of southern Africa, though voluntary separation in many spheres of daily life would no doubt continue for a long time. Provided the law does not compel people to segregate, it is unreasonable to force them to desegregate if they choose to live separately. It would be free to everyone to have exclusive clubs or eating-houses, or to live in suburbs that are—by custom, not by law —exclusive, always provided that public funds are not used to provide such racially exclusive amenities.

These ideas will naturally be gravely disturbing to those whites who are accustomed to segregation, particularly as practised in the northern provinces of the RSA. But the hard fact is that publicly enforced or condoned racial discrimination could have no place in a federation such as is here under consideration. Those who favour federation because they see great advantages in it would naturally do their utmost to ease the transition. But it would be folly to attempt to disguise the fact that racial separation as practised in the RSA would have to go if federation is to come about.

The difficulties of transition would probably not be as formidable as they seem. There is no racial separation of this kind in the three independent states, and until comparatively recent times there was no statutory separation in the Cape Province. Moreover, there are aspects of apartheid that few whites would want to retain. The laws governing mixed marriages and the so-called Immorality Act have few advocates left.[1] Even the pass laws are coming to be seen as anachronistic. In the matter of hotels and restaurants, strict apartheid has been waived by the government itself in the interests of friendly relations with neighbouring states and with the Transkei, and the indications are that this new outlook is spreading. There are many white South Africans who would willingly see considerable, if not total, relaxation of the colour bar in sport. Finally, there are no grounds for regarding colour-bar habits and customs as immutable.

A matter that would require careful handling is that of land-ownership. Laws on this differ from Lesotho, where land is public rather than private, to Botswana and Swaziland where it is both public and private and anyone may own private land, and to the RSA, where it can be privately owned but where there are laws making it illegal for whites to own land in a Bantustan or for Africans to own land in white areas. In the RSA, moreover, there is legislation such as the Group Areas Act that prohibits members of a particular racial group from owning or even occupying property in an urban area not demarcated for that group. As many white South Africans know and affirm there is nothing to be said in favour of retaining the Group Areas Act whose operation has been uni-formly unfair to non-whites. The ordinary land laws, dating in the case of South Africa to the Land Act of 1913 and in the case of Lesotho even further back, are a more difficult matter. This is not because their amendment in order to abolish racial separation might affect large numbers of whites; in practice very few whites would be involved. But the alteration of the laws, if carried out hastily, might lead to inflation of land values and the concentration of land in the hands of fewer and fewer people. This is another matter that cannot be settled on paper but should be left to those called upon to advise the different governments contemplating federation.

It is not difficult to imagine the outcry that would be raised by the suggestion that all apartheid—not merely that enforced by the

---

[1] There is little written evidence for this assertion because people are normally inhibited from the public expression of disagreement about an act blatantly called an Immorality Act. When a flagrant case comes before the courts, however, letters in the Afrikaans and English press bear out the contention that the act is disliked and that few would regret its quiet repeal or disuse. To say so openly however, has come to be tantamount to advocating 'immorality'. The Prohibition of Mixed Marriages Act (1949) prohibits marriage between white and non-white. The Immorality Act of 1927 made extra-marital intercourse between white and African illegal and the amending act of 1950 extended the act to include all non-whites.

patently wrong and useless legislation such as the Immorality Act—
would have to be given up if federation were to come about. Nor
does it serve any purpose, even if it were true, to stigmatize this outcry as white hypocrisy to defend privilege. That is only part of the
truth; but even if it were completely true, the fact remains that the
people who raise the outcry are the white voters whose assent to
federation would be sought. The only way to meet such opposition
is in the first place to show why apartheid is not the economic and
cultural protection that its adherents believe it to be, and, in the
second place, to examine how federation could in fact promote the
security and prosperity now vainly sought behind the walls of racial
separation.

Most of the arguments maintaining that apartheid, regarded as
a 'defence of white civilization', is illusory, are familiar enough and
need only be mentioned here without elaboration. After more than
a century of statutory separation between white and non-white in
the northern provinces of the RSA, and of customary separation in
the Cape Province, and after twenty years of much stricter statutory
racial separation in the whole country, the white adherents of
apartheid do not appear to feel any more secure than before. On the
contrary, they are more uncomfortably aware that the Bantustan
policy has failed signally to turn back the tide of Africans moving
to white urban areas. The ever more stringent laws that have been
placed on the statute book are a sign of white fear; and there seems
to be no other logical end to the process than that the RSA must
become entirely a police state.

Nor has the economy of the country benefited. It has been hampered
by legislation restricting the right to seek employment and to employ.
The cultural values of the whites have become attenuated by growing
isolation as a direct result of apartheid, and some ninety-nine per
cent of the countries of the world have excluded her from many international bodies. The most spectacular of such exclusions is in the
world of sport; but more important are the boycotts of South
Africa in intellectual organizations, and the fear of racism that prevents many intellectuals from seeking work in the RSA and that
drives some of her own intellectuals out. South Africa has many
enemies, not as some foolish people believe because of her wealth,
but because the world today will no longer accept racial discrimination.

It is clear that apartheid can no longer be regarded with any confidence as a protection of 'the white way of life'. Even the Bantu-stans, conceived in the spirit of apartheid, offer no real hope. Nevertheless, it is to the illusion of apartheid that most whites will cling, unless they can be given a practical alternative. If federation is to be considered as such an alternative, its advantages must be clear and present, not some vague, cloudy, and generalized hope for the future. What may we legitimately suppose such advantages to be?

9

ADVANTAGES OF FEDERATION

THE area we are considering has variations in soil and climate that range from tropical to desert. It has mineral resources, great in extent, variety, and quality. It has a long coast line with reasonably good harbours and with large supplies of fish. It is underpopulated with its population unevenly distributed, and it has no inland waterways to provide cheap transport; it has a transport system that is inadequate for its growing needs. Its two chief economic requirements are controlled water supplies to combat periodic drought, and power. It has considerable potential hydro-electric resources.

About forty per cent of the area is desert or scrub, another thirty per cent is agriculturally underdeveloped and misused to the extent that yields tend to diminish, while in many parts of the remaining thirty per cent—chiefly the areas farmed by whites—advanced agriculture is practised. However, because of the poverty of most of the population the internal market for the products of this area is poor, and overseas markets are actively sought and subsidized, thus increasing the local cost of living. Though there are areas where farms are improved from generation to generation, much of South African farming has some of the characteristics of mining whose object is to extract wealth while it lasts.

The underdeveloped areas comprise mainly the Bantustans of the RSA, South-West Africa, and the three independent states of Swaziland, Lesotho, and Botswana. The reasons for their underdevelopment may be some or all of the following: slowness in adapting from a subsistence to a money economy; lack of sufficient land for economic farming; poor transport systems; uncontrolled floods and droughts; the general poverty which means malnutrition and overstocking and closes the door to adequate loans for development; absence of a large proportion of able-bodied males earning a living elsewhere. Whatever the causes, the results are that more than half the area of southern Africa is being wastefully used, thus impoverishing the whole.

The mining and industrial development of South Africa has been so spectacular that it has blinded observers to the retarding effects of the shortage of skilled and unskilled labour and to job reservation legislation which limits the skilled work that non-whites may do. It has, however, not blinded industrialists and mine-owners to these things. They know that progress could be even more spectacular if such legislation was abolished and if the imported labour that is employed came from less entirely foreign sources. South Africa's transport system, too, suffers from this lack of manpower. In the RSA itself there are large areas, chiefly but not solely in the Bantustans, that are ill served by road and rail; and the three independent neighbouring states are even worse off. In them this is not solely due to the lack of manpower but to the need for large capital borrowing and investment which smaller units cannot achieve.

South African harbours are, as I have said, only reasonably good and if the hinterland were to undergo greater economic expansion, as is predicted and is certainly possible, they would be unable to cope with the traffic. The fishing industry is only in its infancy, and so great is the supply of fish off southern African coasts that it could provide the whole of southern Africa with highly nutritious processed food. But there are three conditions: a bigger effective internal market, the transport to reach it, and control to prevent the fishing-grounds from being over-fished.

Controlled water supplies and controlled droughts are two of the greatest needs of southern Africa. To fulfil those needs, flood waters must be controlled for irrigation and, in the process, harnessed to produce cheap industrial power. The rivers suitable for such purposes are the Vaal, the Orange, the Kunene, and the Zambezi. Of these, the Orange and Kunene flow through the territories of three independent states—Lesotho and the RSA in the case of the Orange River, Portugal and the RSA in the case of the Kunene River. Though the Zambezi is not a South African river, the RSA is deeply involved in the hydro-electric scheme at Cabora Bassa, in Moçambique, and will eventually draw more than half its electrical output for industrial use in the RSA.

Nearly one-third of the citizens of South Africa of all races live in urban areas, that is, on less than one per cent of the total area. Half the urban population lives in Johannesburg, Cape Town, and Durban, and of these almost one-third are concentrated on the Witwatersrand area alone, drawn there by the gold-mining industry and the primary and secondary industries that have grown up round it. This industrial concentration has resulted in an imbalance in population distribution as between town and country that, many people feel, could be redressed with healthy results for the country generally.

These facts about the economic underdevelopment of southern Africa are well known to industrial and commercial leaders and it would be necessary for white voters to consider them in asking whether federation would in any way remedy them. All the advantages of federation that existed in 1908, but were disregarded or discarded, exist today, waiting to be seized. There is, moreover, greater urgency to recognize the need for them now than there was in 1908. The need for orderly economic development; the uneven distribution of industry, capital, labour, and thus of population; the need for a rail and road transport system that would serve the whole of southern Africa effectively; the ever-increasing demand for industrial power and controlled water supply; the organization and exploitation of an expanding internal market for agricultural produce; and the need to find a racial *modus vivendi*—all these are questions that are today more urgent than in 1908. To sum up, a way must be found for the peaceful economic development of southern Africa; a way that will neither destroy nor endanger those human values that we associate with smaller, rather than larger, geographical areas; a way of combining central economic planning and development with local cultural autonomy. It is in the tackling of these problems that the advantages of federation for southern Africa should be sought.

A few examples will serve to illustrate this. Since the early 1920s there have been South Africans, the most notable being the late N. J. Havenga,[1] who have been concerned at the depopulation of rural areas and the concentration of population in a few industrial areas. Havenga and others advocated what was popularly called 'decentralization of industry', but when his party came to power in 1924, Havenga was unable to stem the strong economic tide that was producing the conditions he rightly deplored.

Since 1948, successive Nationalist Party governments have tried to give effect to its apartheid policy, which included self-government and ultimate independence for Bantustans, and at the same time the policy of border industries was invented to do two things:

[1] Life-long friend and follower of General J. B. M. Hertzog, Minister of Finance throughout his premiership and, for a short while, under Malan.

reverse the flow of African industrial labour to the cities and create industrial jobs for them nearer home. The policy has in practice failed to do either of these things. It has indeed created new industrial complexes, with high concentration of African population, but these are not so much on the borders of Bantustans as on the borders of existing industrial areas such as Durban, East London, Johannesburg, and Pretoria. Nor has the policy succeeded in stemming the flow to the existing population concentrations such as the Witwatersrand, where the African population has in fact steadily increased. The reason why the policy of border industries has failed, and will continue to fail, to achieve the hoped-for results are, in the first place, that the ideology of apartheid demands that white capital and industry should not be allowed within the Reserves (or future Bantustans),[1] where Africans themselves are presumed to take the lead. In the second place, the ideology was not really concerned with the problems of urban over-population but merely with having too many Africans concentrated there; this, it was considered, represented a danger to the whites. Policies undertaken from mistaken motives are apt to miscarry.

The theory of border industries, like its parent apartheid, is based on fear—fear that the Bantustans might become economic rivals if industries were developed too rapidly within them, and fear of having too many Africans in urban areas. These fears are not unreal. If Bantustans do become independent and have their own industries, they may well be able to undercut South African manufactures; and, as for urban areas, it may be that spending far more money on social amenities for the poorest section, the non-whites, would lessen the chances of racial clashes; but where there are, in an imperfect society, large concentrations of racially different groups, the danger of such clashes is always present.

Nevertheless, the dispersal of industries, properly carried out, could be made to serve desirable social and economic ends. It could bring about the essential economic development of the Bantustans and of Lesotho, Botswana, and Swaziland, and at the same time ease the pressure of population on existing industrial concentrations; it could create a more accessible market for agricultural and ocean products; it would make the provision of better transport to these areas economically sound; and it is arguable that it would ultimately

---

[1] There has been some relaxation in this and 'white' capital may now be invested in the homelands, but only through a government agency.

result in a far more economic use of labour, thus benefiting not only the region concerned but the whole of southern Africa.

While such advantages cannot be achieved by a policy of industrial dispersal that is conceived and carried out in terms of the ideology of apartheid, based as this is on fear rather than on clearly understood objectives, it is possible that they may be achieved by federation which would have the clearly conceived aims mentioned in the previous paragraph. An autonomous Transkei or Zululand or Botswana, federally united to some fourteen other regions in southern Africa, ceases to be a threat to the white voters of the RSA and becomes an asset. Central economic planning for the whole of southern Africa with its diversity of conditions would become possible under federation; but the cultural and political autonomy of the regions would be retained much more effectively than at present. Southern Africa would, in fact, become an economic unity with greatly increased borrowing powers, greater strength in trading and commercial relations with other countries, and greater ability to participate in the development of the rest of Africa. Such a southern African federation, wishing to become an associate member of the European Common Market, would be much more readily acceptable than would its present unco-ordinated parts.[1]

An example of the kind of difficulty that at present hampers the RSA as well as her neighbours is the Cabora Bassa hydro-electric scheme in Moçambique. This is on Portuguese territory but will closely affect its neighbours, of which the RSA is the largest. Indeed, without the capital and expertise of South Africa (among other countries) and particularly without her undertaking to buy more than half the power output, it is doubtful whether the project can be successfully completed. In 1970 Zambia and other states were objecting to the scheme, partly because a portion of the power output will benefit Rhodesia, but largely because of the fear that this is merely another example of expanding South African imperialism—an attempt to spread white domination and apartheid beyond her

[1] The RSA still enjoys some of the preferential treatment that members of the Commonwealth do. She belongs to the Sterling Area and is thus exempt from the Exchange Control Act (1947) of Britain which severely limits British investment in non-sterling area countries. Furthermore, many of her imports enjoy preference in Britain, Australia, Canada, and New Zealand. Sooner or later, however, other members of the Commonwealth are bound to agitate for the discontinuance of these privileges. In such matters, Britain and the Commonwealth would probably view a federation of southern Africa in a different light from that in which it regards the RSA.

borders. Already two European countries have, under pressure from African states, withdrawn permission for their manufacturers to supply materials, and two more are under heavy pressure to do so. There is little doubt that, if ideological considerations are excluded, the Cabora Bassa scheme would benefit southern Africa immensely. There is equally little doubt that ideological considerations will not be excluded. But if the RSA became part of a federation such as we have been considering, criticism and talk of the extension of white domination would become meaningless.[1] The white voters of the RSA—for it is they whom we are at present considering—would gain an immense advantage without endangering themselves or anyone else. The abandonment of the illusory protection of apartheid seems a small price for them to pay for the immense advantages of being able to participate in the development of Africa and to be able to do so freely, without being suspected of ulterior motives and without endangering their own 'separateness'.

When South Africa was a Dominion and a member of the Commonwealth the argument was frequently used that she would never be able to expand to greatness as long as she was, if not subservient, at least attached to Great Britain. The impetus needed was independence, the establishment of a republic, and in support of this argument the example of the USA was quoted. While the thirteen colonies were under Britain they were small and struggling, their economies tied to that of the mother country; but once they broke the ties all bars to progress were removed, and within 150 years the United States became the wealthiest and most powerful country in the Western world.

This argument is fallacious. South Africa lacks many of the geographic advantages that enabled the USA to exploit its wealth—great navigable rivers and its position between East and West. Nor did South Africa at any stage adopt the immigration policy that gave the USA millions of citizens from Europe. In time, South Africa did become a republic, but it is doubtful if her economic progress has been greater since 1961 than it would have been had she remained a member of the Commonwealth. There is, however, a sense in which a comparison with the USA may well be made. It is arguable—and the Founding Fathers of the United States would almost certainly have so argued—that what gave the real impetus

---

[1] It is true that Zambia's objection about Rhodesia would remain, but that is a separate question that cannot be dealt with here.

to the spectacular growth of the USA was not separation from the mother country but the subsequent federation of the thirteen states. It is not sovereign independence that will make for the economic progress of Lesotho, Botswana, Swaziland, and the RSA. Independence may well be a prerequisite, but it is in a federal association that southern Africa is more likely to enjoy greater economic prosperity.

White voters, when considering the pros and cons of federation, might be inclined to argue that there may be advantages but that all these will accrue to the Black states and will have to be paid for by the whites. Speaking about the neighbouring states of the RSA, Mr. Anton Rupert, the South African industrialist, said: 'If they don't eat, how can we sleep?' He was expressing an economic as well as a philosophical truth. It is coming to be accepted that an economic system in which the rich nations become richer and the poor nations poorer, is doomed. Somehow the widening gap must be bridged and this cannot be done by sending gifts of food in times of famine, however much they alleviate present hunger and soothe the consciences of wealthy nations. The USA has found that it can no longer sell all that it can produce, and that it is futile to give the 'surplus' away. This is probably the overriding problem of the modern world, and white South Africans are not exempt from it. Whatever the solution may prove to be, there is considerable truth in the frequently expressed apology for apartheid that 'we believe in helping people to help themselves'. This is sound policy, but the trouble is that, under apartheid, South African whites carry it out in a half-hearted, hit-and-miss manner that brings advantages to no one.

An instance of this is the policy of Bantustans. Theoretically this involves the creation of self-governing Bantu homelands that will ultimately become independent. This policy is hampered at every turn. Many white voters, possibly even a majority, regard it as fragmenting South Africa. Others object to spending so-called 'white' money on black territories. Others, again, flatly disbelieve that the Bantustans will ever be allowed to become truly independent because they would then constitute too serious a security risk for the whites. Above all, the rest of the world is sceptical and regards the Bantustan policy as a trick by which the white rulers of the RSA hope to retain both power and privilege, to have all the supposed advantages without any of the opprobium that attaches to racial discrimination.

All these criticisms of apartheid, as at present conceived and carried out, are justified. As is the case with border industries, this aspect of apartheid has failed and will continue to fail as long as it is regarded as a reason for depriving more than half the African population of citizenship rights in white areas, where they live permanently, on the grounds that they can exercise those rights in their own homelands. It is well known that, on the most optimistic calculations, the present homelands will never be able to provide a living for more than about one-third of the African population. Yet, properly conceived, there is merit in the idea of Bantustans as there is in the decentralizing of industry. Conceived of as autonomous units in a federation of some fifteen autonomous regions they become a more convincing reality. Their creation would remove from many white people in the RSA the fear of the existing stark proportions. 'They outnumber us by five to one' need no longer exercise a kind of fascinating fear over the minds of white people. There will, of course, still be non-whites in all regions, because federation is not a method a separating the races, of realizing the ideal of some people for a partitioning of South Africa. But in no autonomous region could the interests of one group dominate over the rights of another.

It is now generally accepted that racial prejudice is indeed prejudice. It exists but is not inherited, and it manifests itself in all kinds of fears and animosities between groups, particularly where one greatly outnumbers the other. This prejudice is not inherited but is of course transmitted from one generation to the next and it grows by what it feeds on. Yet there are plenty of examples of individuals who have freed themselves from this particular kind of thraldom. Throughout the world, men and women are preoccupied with this problem that threatens to engulf mankind and they are trying to find out the best ways to combat it. Racial prejudice seems to be evoked by anything 'foreign' and to be most virulent where skin colour clearly marks out the foreign element. Whether people with so-called 'white' skins are more prejudiced than those with coloured or black skins it would be hard to say. The whole phenomenon appears to be a comparatively recent one (speaking in historical centuries) and to be not unconnected with the feelings of superiority of a conquering group. It may also be closely associated with differences in economic status between races. It is possible that racial prejudice may be the manifestation of deeper psychological factors such as feelings of guilt and sexual jealousy. It also seems to be closely associated with fear, but possibly this, too, is a manifestation of deeper causes.

No one knows how racial prejudice can be prevented from destroying the very fabric of society in the USA and in the RSA, to mention only two countries. It is not much use confining ourselves to hoping that, in the long run, reason and common economic and cultural interests will drive out fear and prejudice; anyone who believes that man is educable will believe that such hopes are not vain. Nevertheless, common sense would dictate that practical steps to hasten the realization of hopes could be taken now and that one such step might be to reduce the pressures of race upon race—not by artificially separating them for part of the 24-hour day into white, black, and Coloured group areas—but by trying to remove the fears that non-whites have of hunger, of economic want, of white domination, and that whites have of black 'swamping' or domination. Both sets of fears are real and they are almost identical.

Fear of economic want is being fostered rather than eliminated by South Africa's racial policies. It was said earlier that federation would involve the disappearance of apartheid as it is known today. It is now suggested that the kind of federation here proposed might reduce the pressure of fear that keeps racial prejudice in all its forms active. If there is a correlation between racial prejudice and inequality of numbers, federation would, it was pointed out, reduce the inequality over most parts of the proposed federation. Moreover, the release of economic energy that might well be brought about by federation would enable the people of southern Africa to tackle another root of prejudice—economic want—with greater hope of success. It may be objected that federation in the United States has apparently not brought about such desirable results. This is a shallow view of present-day racial violence in the USA; that springs from a variety of social and economic causes which feed the racial prejudice that dates back to slavery and the domination of white over black. A federal system of government is not a panacea for all ills. In itself it will no more cure apartheid or racial prejudice in the USA than it will cure cancer. It cannot even be claimed that it is some mythical form of 'best' government. All that is claimed is that in certain circumstances, such as those in the United States and in southern Africa, it is more likely to provide the conditions required for an orderly way of life. Racial prejudice is powerful. It will not be driven out by violence that will only substitute one form of prejudice for another. It will not be subdued by laws alone, though laws, as in the USA, are an essential part of the machinery to contain it. It will not be rooted out by constitutional forms alone; but one constitutional form may be more suited than another to control it. In the case of the USA, the most devastating of all forms of human prejudice, that of slavery, was abolished only after a civil war that came close to destroying the state itself. It is arguable that, had her constitution not been federal, the United States would not have survived the Civil War.

We must now turn to the effect on world opinion of the acceptance by the South African electorate of federation. An Afrikaans journalist once said that South Africa was the 'polecat of the world'. Her racial policies stank in the post-Hitler world. Volumes could be written about existing discrimination on grounds of sex, religion, and caste in all parts of the world, even to the ultimate degradation of slavery. But the world, careless as it may be about discrimination in general, has grown extremely sensitive about racial discrimination. While there are many parts of the world where gross racial discrimination occurs, in the RSA it is embedded in the constitution and in a great number of laws passed by a white parliament. In other countries racial discrimination continues to operate in spite of the laws against it. In the RSA it operates because of the laws— it is discrimination by act of parliament.

Apartheid is the epitome of racial discrimination and its results are devastating. In order to put it into practice many of the laws of economics and considerations of humanity have to be flouted. Freedom to seek work is denied to millions of men who, to make a living, must perforce live separately from their families. Apartheid has been elevated to the status of an ideology, and any government whose policies must conform strictly to that will have to suppress opposition. This has happened in South Africa where there are laws that enable a Minister to ban individuals, commit them to house arrest, hold them in solitary confinement, without legal warrant and denying them access to the courts. In many countries the rule of law is neglected or thrust aside at executive convenience. In South Africa it has been breached by act of parliament.

While all the evils that may exist in South Africa must not be attributed to apartheid, there is a strong connection between it and the fact that a majority of South African citizens live below the bread line, that poverty, disease, infant mortality, and the diseases that result from malnutrition are rife. A great many white South Africans do not know these facts but the rest of the world knows enough about them to make it deny to South Africa full participation in official and unofficial world organizations. The world includes more than a hundred states, and, as many South Africans have pointed out, in many of these, all stern critics of the RSA, even worse conditions of hunger and poverty prevail. It is a fruitless argument. Hunger and want in India or some parts of the USA neither excuses nor alleviates hunger and want in the RSA.

There can be no doubt that apartheid has made South Africa internationally unpopular and that most white South Africans are aware of this. There is also little doubt that most of them would welcome a way out of their difficulties. It is facile, but not very helpful, to say that the matter is really quite simple: all that white South Africa has to do is to abandon apartheid forthwith. What has been said in this book points to the complexity of the situation and supports the view that it is naïve to expect white South Africans to relinquish part of their power and privilege unless alternative policies can be found that would guarantee—not power and privilege, for that would merely be fraud—but those very fundamental rights which they are themselves at present denying to others. It is submitted that this can never be done under present constitutional arrangements in southern Africa, and that a federal structure is a more hopeful alternative.

It would be ingenuous to invest the word federation with some inherent magic that will make all the rough places smooth. It would be foolish to imagine that a federal structure would be immediately effective in 'solving' problems or that it would immediately be hailed by world opinion as a sign that white South Africans had, at a stroke, abolished apartheid. Whether a federation of southern Africa can be made to work must depend on the ingenuity and practical common sense of those who make the constitution and on the goodwill of all southern Africans. Whether the world would accept such a federal arrangement as indicating a real change of direction would naturally depend on the constitution and on the voting of the people concerned. The world would want assurances that the constitutional safeguards were real and that racial discrimination was on its way out.

World opinion about South Africa and apartheid has been

formed over twenty years and will not quickly change. South Africa's critics will be sceptical about the leopard changing his spots. Nevertheless, if federation can be seen to be based on principles other than apartheid, her friends will no longer be able to do nothing but make half-hearted and shamefaced excuses for her. The RSA has strong friends at the UN whose hands are to a large extent tied. Given solid grounds for the belief that federation means a clear departure from racial discrimination, those friends would be able to defend a southern African federation of which South Africa was a part. Through the federation, white South Africans would be reconciled with world opinion.

One aspect of the problem that has only been touched on is the reaction of world opinion to the inclusion of South-West Africa either as a single region or as two regions of a federation of which a partitioned RSA would form part. Despite the scorn with which many white South Africans profess to treat the UN, they must perforce pay attention to it. They may regard the UN as a collection of noisy small nations most of whom are physically unable to carry out their dire threats against apartheid and depend on the great powers to do so for them. The fact is that the UN remains, and is likely to remain, the focus of world opinion. White South Africans like to believe that the great powers 'don't really believe in all that UN nonsense but have to pretend so as to keep the small nations sweet'. But, in fact, world opinion, reflected back from the UN, does influence the decisions of most governments. Few nations would, for instance, openly defy the application of sanctions to Rhodesia or continue to license the export of arms to the RSA, and the decisions to apply sanctions are taken by sovereign independent states at the instance of the UN. So-called world opinion about racial discrimination can thus be formed at the UN and result in action at the national level. It can also be formed at a national level when the people of a country themselves feel so strongly about racial discrimination that, without international prompting, they will refuse to have official or unofficial dealings with the country that practises it. In this way, most African states refuse to have diplomatic relations with the RSA and discourage trade with her.

Botswana, Swaziland, and Lesotho are independent states and if they were asked to consider going into a federation with other states, the decision would be theirs alone. The case of South-West Africa is, of course, different. If a federation were to include

South-West Africa without consultation with the UN, it is improbable that that body would accept it as a *fait accompli* and renounce all say in Namibia. The position of southern Africa would then not have improved. Indeed, the position would be worse than before because other territories would now have become involved in the dispute with the UN about Namibia.

The advantages that a federal solution holds in this matter are considerable, and it would be a mark of sound and mature statesmanship to seek UN approval. Given that, the territory itself would be released from its present state of uncertainty which, if continued, is bound to hamper her development. Southern Africa would be relieved of the haunting fear that some precipitate action by the UN or by African states might give rise to a race war. And the world would be relieved of a vexatious situation that, while it continues, poisons international relations, threatens world peace, and prevents the very thing which sensible people ask for—the progressive development of South-West Africa for the benefit of its inhabitants. These happy results might well accrue if white South Africans were to accept a genuinely non-discriminatory federal constitution and were to swallow national pride and seek permission from the UN. This would be a delicate task in which the good offices of some of the great powers might well be sought. But delicate and difficult as the operation would be, the prize would be great, and the penalty for failure will also be great, for white South Africans no less than for non-white.

The questions we have been considering—Bantustans, border industries, apartheid—cannot be dealt with in isolation because all interact on one another. Still less can the question of national defence be isolated. The nature and extent of the defence problem that would face a federation are affected by every one of the aspects already referred to in this and previous chapters.

We saw in Chapter 5 that, between 1910 and 1945, South Africa's armed forces had been used twice in world wars and a number of times in maintaining internal security. Since 1948 they had been employed on internal security and, in recent years, on the defence of the RSA's borders against guerrilla infiltration. We saw, too, that the nature and extent of South Africa's defence problems had changed since 1910, partly as a result of her leaving the Commonwealth and partly as a result of her racial policies. In seeking to compare the nature of those problems under federation with what they are at present we must bear in mind that we are really comparing the defence of the RSA with that of a southern African federation. White South Africans will naturally ask themselves whether a federation would give them greater security, make them more valuable, and thus acceptable, as allies in war, and what effect it would have on the taxes they have to pay. In other words, what advantages would federation hold for them in this respect?

The objects of defence policy in a southern African federation would presumably be to secure from outside attack some thousands of miles of coastline stretching from the Angolan border on the Atlantic, round the Cape, to the Moçambique border on the Indian Ocean; to secure the defence of some further thousands of miles of land frontiers bordering on Angola, Zambia, Rhodesia, and Moçambique; to provide internal security in peace and war; and to make sure that supplies of men and materials and of food are available in time of war. One of the objects of foreign policy would be to promote the objects of defence policy, both in the matter of supplies and of seeking alliances in case of war.

In purely naval terms, the coastal defence of a southern African federation would not be essentially different from that of the RSA. Sitting astride the Cape route, no southern African government could remain neutral in a world war; but that is the only kind of war in which her coastline is likely to be threatened—she could never, alone, defend herself against attack by a major power, but such an attack would immediately spark off a world war. Southern African policy would therefore be not to cripple itself by trying to build up a great navy—a task that will always be beyond its resources—but to choose allies. In the prevailing alignment of world powers there is little doubt that, since neutrality is not possible, southern Africa would choose what are known as the Western powers. This would mean the navies of the USA, Britain, France, and India, the strongest naval force in the Indian Ocean. It would be with these navies that southern African coastal defence would have to co-operate.

While the problem would thus not have been materially altered, the means of dealing with it would undergo radical change. Since we must assume that the federation would have the approval of most countries, more particularly of its probable allies in time of war, foreign policy and the supply of naval and military material would be immensely eased. The present acrimonious bickering about Simonstown would cease because the position of the dockyard would fall into proper perspective. Southern Africa would not feel the need, as the RSA does now, to shop around for armaments because Britain and the Commonwealth dislike her racial policies. Those policies would have been generally approved otherwise the federation would hardly have come into existence. Nor would her future allies feel the need to be cautious in committing themselves to an alliance with her as they now are to a country whose racial policies are universally abhorred.

The problem of the defence of the land frontiers of the federation would also be simplified. They would be almost halved in extent, and the ever-present danger of a race war in southern Africa that now haunts military advisers and Ministers of Defence, as it does many other people, will be greatly diminished and, one might legitimately hope, will disappear altogether in a reasonably brief time. African states that now might, if they could, attack the RSA in order to liberate their fellow Africans from white domination would find it difficult to convince others that a federation to which three independent African states adhered, and in the constitution of which the policy of racial discrimination had been, as it were, dissolved, was white-dominated or that it constituted a threat to world peace.

Leading South African politicians and statesmen have laid great stress on the dangers of Communism in a multi-racial society. These dangers are real, more especially because of the appeal that a doctrine which, in theory at any rate, abolishes racial discrimination has for those who suffer under it. In a country in which practically all legislation discriminates against non-whites it would be remarkable if they did not find Communism a less unhappy doctrine than do their rulers. The possibility has to be faced that some or all of the states north of a southern African federation may embrace elements of Communist practice, possibly with the aid of China rather than that of Russia.

This possibility becomes greater when it is borne in mind that the regimes of Rhodesia and Portugal are containing their non-white citizens by force of arms, and that substantial numbers of technicians from Communist China are building the Tanzania–Zambia railway. The dangers to a southern African federation, therefore, as to the RSA, of infiltration and even of outright war cannot be discounted. In both eventualities, infiltration or outright war, a federation of southern Africa would be better off than the RSA in two respects: the length of border to be defended would have been reduced and the problem of internal security would have been lessened if not eliminated.

At present, internal security would be a very great problem indeed in a global war. The Communist countries against which the RSA would be aligned would obviously direct their propaganda towards inciting non-whites to revolt or to refuse to co-operate in the war effort, and her ability to fight alongside her allies would be considerably reduced. There is little doubt that the likelihood of this influences Western powers in their present relations with the RSA. A high proportion of her white armed forces would be engaged in keeping non-whites at bay; and while a federation might not immediately eleminate this danger, it would undoubtedly reduce to normal proportions the number of men required to maintain internal security during wartime.

While the RSA is by no means economically self-sufficient she is reasonably independent of foreign supplies in most things except certain types of armament. She would even, as in two previous wars, be able to supply her allies. Nevertheless, a long war would strain her economic resources unless she had outside aid. Her ability to support herself would be diminished by the demands of internal security, and her ability to stockpile during peacetime has been decreased by international disinclination to assist a country that discriminates on grounds of race.

In order to assure herself of adequate and continuous supplies of military and naval armaments she must have as her allies friendly disposed nations. In present circumstances it is no easy task to find these, as her Foreign Ministers and ambassadors have found. There are, indeed, friendly nations that are anxious to increase trade with the RSA and to draw her more closely into the trade and defence orbit of Western Europe and the USA; but they find their efforts baulked by her racial policies that expose to both internal and foreign difficulties those states that are prepared to ignore apartheid. South Africa may improve her trade relations with her small neighbours who are economically dependent on her, but the far more important markets of Africa and the world will become more difficult to exploit and, in wartime, impossible.

A further point to be considered under the head of defence is the control, organization, and composition of the armed forces in a federation. In the whole area of southern Africa to which we are giving attention only the RSA has armed forces—air, military, naval. Her defence force consists of a permanent force and a large part-time citizen force of citizens subject to compulsory military training. They are all white, although there are non-white men in the armed forces in a menial capacity.

The policy of the RSA is to keep complete control over all armed forces and apply racial discrimination in every branch. The question is what the federal policy would be, and it is a question which, if not effectively answered, will make federation impossible. White control of all armed forces would, in actual practice, not be any different for the non-white population of the RSA and for the three independent African states whose security from outside attack is, even now, tightly bound to that of the RSA. But this argument can hardly be expected to appeal to the non-whites and, even if their opposition could be overcome, world opinion would almost certainly regard such a federation as a method of perpetuating white supremacy. In any case, it would be highly undesirable to establish a federation on such a basis because it undermines the very principles that might recommend federation to all races.

The question is one that can be answered only by the people and the states concerned. But one or two points may be suggested here merely to indicate, in the first place, that the problem is by no means hopeless and, secondly, that the advantages of federation to white South Africans in the matter of defence alone would be so great that they should think carefully before rejecting it outright.

In existing circumstances, white fears in the RSA are understandable and difficult to remove. But it is justifiable to hope that some at least of the fears that inspire apartheid will be removed by federation. Other countries, too, have had the problem of race fear and prejudice in their armed forces and have made, and are making, efforts to overcome them. South Africa has herself experimented with separate regiments, particularly at the training stage, and she and other countries similarly placed have much to learn from one another. It was pointed out earlier that a large part of the work of the armed forces has in the past been to deal with internal security—in plain language, possible revolt. Under a reasonable federal system much of this would fall away and might possibly be left to fully fledged army units based on regions but federally controlled.

Constitutional control of the armed forces would obviously be a crucial point. This might be so vested as to make it virtually impossible in peacetime for one racial group in the federation or in a region to obtain legal domination over another by means of a *coup d'état*. There is only one answer to the old argument, that 'human nature being what it is', what we have to guard against is not legal, but illegal means. The reply is that it is obviously sensible, in framing a constitution as in all else, to take reasonable precautions, but that 'human nature being what it is', it is a waste of time to discuss a federal constitution on the basis that there is no longer any trust left between people or states. Constitutional safeguards there must be against racial discrimination and the domination of one race by another, but unless there is some mutual trust the safeguards will in any case be useless. A federal constitution can go a long way towards securing these aims, but in the end we have always to fall back on human nature as it is.

In the matter of defence the advantages of federation for the whites of the RSA no less than for the remaining eighteen million people are great. National defence would take on an entirely different aspect. National security, now a bugbear, could be obtained for a fraction of the present costs. The problem of supplies and allies would be no more than normal. The path of foreign policy would be smoothed, and the relaxation of racial tensions in southern Africa would be dramatic. The reply, therefore, to white taxpayers who want assurances is that it would result in far greater security, would make southern Africa once more an acceptable ally, and would have these results at considerably less than the taxpayer of the RSA is today called upon to provide.

10

HOW FEDERATION COULD HAPPEN

THE argument of this book has been that present policies in the
RSA and South-West Africa can lead only to stagnation or to racial
conflict which would be difficult to contain. It was suggested that
a federation of southern Africa might provide a way that would
avoid both stagnation and conflict, and that such a federation could
consist of some fifteen autonomous regions comprising the eleven
into which the RSA would be partitioned together with Lesotho,
Swaziland, Botswana, and Namibia. The advantages and disadvantages of this have been discussed in relation to the different regions
and to different racial groups.

In order to prevent the discussion from remaining in the air, I have
outlined the general form of such a federation, but at various stages
have pointed out that not only was it not intended to provide a blueprint for federation but that it was impossible and, indeed, undesirable to attempt to do so. As a result, many questions to which answers
are important have had to be touched on briefly only or mentioned
only to be relegated for formulation and decision by the representatives of the people ultimately concerned—that is, the twenty-two
million inhabitants of southern Africa. It is worth while referring
briefly to one or two instances of matters that had to be omitted
altogether, to show both how important they are and why they could
not be fruitfully discussed here.

The first is that of the composition of the regional and central
legislatures and the form of their executives. Some people believe
that a bicameral system is better than a unicameral, or that a presidential-type executive, such as in the USA, is preferable to the parliamentary-type of the RSA and the Transkei. These are obviously
important questions, but they must equally obviously be left to be
decided by constitutional conferences. Provided that the essential
features of a federation are not breached—autonomous regions,
sound fiscal arrangements, a bill of rights, and an independent
judiciary to safeguard the constitution—it would not matter much

to which type of legislature or executive the final decision went. Moreover, these are not questions on which constitutional conferences are likely to split irrevocably, thus preventing federation from coming about at all.

This may not, however, be true of the next example, namely, franchise qualifications. It will be recalled that this question nearly prevented union in 1908 and was resolved by a compromise by which franchise qualifications remained as they were before union, which meant that non-whites were entirely excluded in the two ex-republics, practically excluded in Natal, and only in the Cape did they retain the vote on a common roll. Subsequently they were deprived of even that right. It is hardly necessary to say that such a compromise would be out of the question today for it would mean that, for the federal parliament, all adults in Lesotho, Swaziland, and Botswana, all black adults in the Transkei, and all white adults elsewhere—but no one else—would have the vote! The suggestion has only to be stated to be dismissed. This is a matter in which there may to be a compromise, but it would have to be based on a common roll. Anything else would be rejected by a majority of the inhabitants of southern Africa no less than by the world.

While, again, this is not the place to put forward proposals in any detail, a few remarks may be made and readers left to draw their own conclusions. Dealing with the federal parliament first, the number of representatives elected to parliament by a region would presumably be in proportion to the population of that region. However the RSA may be partitioned, therefore, there would still be some six million non-white as against 1·6 million white voters and, if federation were proposed, the fears of white voters would loom large. However much the country is split up, non-whites will still be in a majority of about six to one in the federation as a whole. Several arguments can be advanced why this need not spell the end of the whites in South Africa. They are an indispensable element in the proposed federation, both economically and politically, and it is highly improbable that the majority of non-whites would want to reduce their importance. There are other parts of southern Africa, as well as further north, where power has been dispersed from white to white-plus-non-white without endangering the position of the whites. Furthermore, any move to use black power to deprive whites of power and rights could be blocked by the constitution with its bill of rights. All in all, the position of whites as a minority in a federation would be far healthier and more secure than under a unitary system with existing policies.

In this connection it might be well to explore the advantages of a qualified common franchise for an area as large as southern Africa and with such cultural and economic diversity. The argument against this has been that it enables a white minority to entrench itself against a non-white majority by heavily qualifying the franchise; but as soon as the non-whites begin to reach the higher qualifications in substantial numbers—enough to appear as a 'threat' to the whites—the minority uses its entrenched position to raise the qualifications. This is what happened in South Africa. In a federation, however, a qualified franchise would be protected by the constitution. And entrenchment in a rigid federal constitution is a different matter from the spurious entrenchment (as it has turned out to be) in a flexible unitary constitution.

All this is not to say that a franchise that clearly aims at limiting the present legislative influence of one race is desirable. But, with three provisos, there may not be sufficient disadvantages in a qualified franchise to warrant wrecking the chances of federation. The provisos are, first, that the qualifications are common and not based on race or sex or religion. In the second place, that they are not subject to alteration at the discretion of a racial minority. And thirdly, that the rights and liberties of any individual who does not qualify for the federal franchise should in no way whatsoever be prejudiced because of that.

In regions where one racial group is in an overwhelming majority, universal adult franchise for regional elections might well find acceptance. In those where there is a fairly equal division of the races the old fears of racial domination might prevail. As with the federal franchise—and with the same provisos—there would seem to be no valid argument against a qualified franchise. There is one final word: in considering this question in relation to the suggested federation of southern Africa, it is possible to be flexible without abandoning long-cherished beliefs, and it is both possible and desirable not to let phrases such as white supremacy and one-man-one-vote impose themselves too rigorously on the mind. As they are used today these two phrases have been robbed of much of their significance. Though they do have a more real meaning, they now bear a distorted meaning and are not only unhelpful but frequently a serious obstacle to understanding.

A third point that was but briefly touched upon was the actual partition of the RSA and the new boundaries of the autonomous regions. The usual trap set for anyone who suggests the partition of a country is to be asked to produce a map. The unwary fall into the trap and then have their map as well as their arguments demolished. The reason for not producing a map or even suggesting boundaries is perfectly sound: these can only be put before the voters by their representatives and only then after prolonged discussion and bargaining and on the advice of scientific experts. To produce a blueprint in advance would be to draw as many red herrings across the trail as there are new boundaries. It might be that the existing boundaries between the RSA and her neighbours would be amicably adjusted. It would certainly be easier under partition/federation to alter the sizes of the existing Bantustans, to their advantage and to the loss of no other region. These two operations, I suggest, would be facilitated by the very fact that the end objective is a federation that unites all the regions. The bargaining can in no way be compared to the land grabbing that normally succeeds war or rebellion.

Akin to this is the difficult question of the rights of a region to opt out of the federation. The war between the states in the USA was fought over this issue, though it was sparked off by the question of the abolition of slavery. A majority of people in the South maintained that their states had the right to leave the union and they actually proclaimed themselves independent, uniting in a Confederacy to fight the war against the North. Lincoln, followed by the majority of the Northerners, denied the right of the South to secede, and these two opposing views were settled in one of the bitterest civil wars in history. It ended in victory for those who maintained that the USA could not be dissolved, but to this day—and possibly even more in this day—the question still vexes and perplexes American citizens. The Central African Federation, on the other hand, was amicably dissolved within a comparatively short time because it was fairly obvious that it could not be held together. Other of the newer federations have had similar experience. Clearly, a federation of southern Africa should not be entered into on the assumption that, after a few years' trial, any region would be free to opt out and, in effect, destroy the structure of the federation. Nevertheless, it would be unwise to set up a federation that could be dissolved only after a long and bitter war. This is a problem that would have to be faced by the statesmen of southern Africa.

A fourth omission, and my final example, is that the suggested federation would not include Malawi, Moçambique, Zambia, and Rhodesia, all of which might legitimately be regarded as part of southern Africa. There is a simple reason for this. Despite the fact that, in 1908, the Transvaal wanted Moçambique included in discussions leading to union, it and Angola are Portuguese colonies and could not be invited to join a federation with a number of autonomous regions. Rhodesia is a country whose legal status is neither secure nor internationally recognized and she is under sanctions by UN decision. She is regarded by all the Commonwealth countries south of the Zambezi as in rebellion against Britain, and they would hardly consider joining a federation with her. Finally, in present circumstances, international approval would not be forthcoming for a federation that included Rhodesia. Malawi and Zambia have, as indeed do the other territories, close links with the south, but they present peculiar problems in the context of a federation, and it seemed better to concentrate on the more straightforward prospects where the problems are complicated and delicate enough without introducing further complications. Relations between the parts of southern Africa we have been considering and Malawi, Zambia, and the two Portuguese colonies are reasonably satisfactory and nothing need interfere with that after federation. If, by the time federation had become a live issue, circumstances had radically altered, the matter would obviously have to be reconsidered. Relations with Rhodesia are not satisfactory in the sense that both Portugal and the RSA openly disregard sanctions imposed by the UN against her. This would certainly be a serious difficulty in the path of Lesotho, Swaziland, and Botswana (as members of the Commonwealth), and might be a decisive objection to international recognition of the proposed federation. This situation, too, may well change.

These are a few only of the questions that have had to be omitted from what is not intended to be a blueprint but, rather, a very general view of what the nature of a federation of southern Africa might be. The time has now come to ask how such a federation could come about. For this to happen there would have to be a popular demand. Leaders of parties with some hope of achieving office would not commit themselves or their parties until they had generated a sufficiently strong public demand. The word 'generated' is used for, on an issue of this nature, public demand is not likely to arise spontaneously as it might, for instance, over the question of the cost of living; and even then it is usually stimulated and focused by a few people. Men and women, in and out of recognized political parties, who were themselves convinced that federation was desirable would presumably form organizations to propagate their ideas and to persuade the political parties to take them under their wing. A constitutional change of such magnitude would disturb vested interests and call for a rearrangement of loyalties. It is generally painful and usually demands higher taxes. It is seldom voluntary, but rather the result of great pressures—growth of population, strategic needs, revolutionary changes in technology or economics—pressures that are resisted as long as possible though the final agreement is often rapid.[1]

Once a movement of this kind is under way the speed with which it grows to the stage where a considerable public demand does exist will depend on political and economic circumstances. A time may come when the disadvantages of existing constitutional arrangements seem suddenly to come into focus, when the man-in-the-street quite readily grasps what is involved, and popular imagination is stirred to demand change. The arrival of such a time may be precipitated by a threat of economic disaster, such as the breakdown of industrial activity through water and power shortages that can be remedied only by close collaboration with neighbouring states; or by economic depression aggravated by prolonged drought.[2] The point may be reached by the threat of war or of serious racial conflict.

It is possible that a combination of disasters may have such serious international significance that diplomatic pressure would be brought to bear on the states of southern Africa to join together rather than fight. Such intervention by the great powers has happened before now and in many parts of the world. It is part of the technique of trying to prevent large-scale war. The RSA's overwhelming economic and military strength may make a race war in southern Africa seem unlikely at the present time. But it is a central theme of this book that such a race war is possible, and this is, of course, firmly in the minds of those concerned with defence. If it does come about, even if it were on the verge of coming about, can anyone doubt that

---

[1] See Macmahon, ed., *Federalism—Mature and Emergent*, Chapter 14, by John Fischer.

[2] The gold standard crisis in the early thirties brought about dramatic changes in South African politics.

it would constitute a threat to the peace of Africa and of the world? And can anyone doubt that the major powers would exert every effort to avoid it? Such a shotgun federation is, however, far from desirable. It would be much better if the modern equivalent of the Selborne Memorandum of 1907 were to precipitate a movement for federation—in this case before fratricidal war rather than after it.

Once the point of a clamorous popular demand for new constitutional arrangements had been reached, political parties would respond quickly. Thereafter, the shape and speed of the movement would depend increasingly on the kind of leadership available. It is at this stage that, it may be expected, exploratory talks would begin. The biggest constitutional operation would be in the RSA where, as we have seen, there would have to be partition/federation and then federation with neighbouring states. One might hazard a guess at the general shape that exploratory talks and subsequent conferences might take, first for the RSA alone and then with Swaziland, Botswana, and Lesotho. It would probably be necessary, before committees of experts could be set to work, to have at least a preliminary delimitation of regions as a basis for their work. Neither a judicial committee, such as the parliamentary delimitation commissions, nor a parliamentary commission on which the government of the day has a majority, would really be suitable. What would be required would be something in the nature of a small all-party commission, possibly nominated by the Speaker of the House of Assembly and the President of the Senate, and served by a secretariat, to draw up working documents for a larger commission on which non-parliamentarians would be included.

It is this larger commission that would have to come to a preliminary agreement about the number, size, and population of the regions-to-be, and its composition would be of great importance. There would certainly have to be representatives of industry, commerce, mining, farming, the professions, and organized labour, as well as people included because of their eminence. But the delimitation of regions would not be a matter that concerned white voters only, and it would be essential to include the chief Ministers of the Transkei and Zululand, African leaders in other possible Bantustans, a Coloured leader, and an Asian leader. Although this might sound like an unwieldy body, there are techniques to enable conferences of this kind to work smoothly and efficiently.

This matter of non-white participation is vital and it may be

necessary for the government of the day to reconsider the bans (if
they still exist) on non-white organizations such as the African
National Congress and, if necessary, to remove the ban on individual
leaders and even to release leaders from gaol. The influence of these
men and women was largely in urban areas and it would not be
much use conferring with either rural or urban Africans without
their recognized leaders. There are, of course, precedents in the rest
of Africa for releasing leaders from gaol to enable them to take
part in constitutional talks, and it is the boast of Afrikaner nationalism that many of its leaders served sentences in prison for political
offences or had been in internment camps during war. There is, too,
a significant difference between the proposed federation conferences
and the negotiations that took place in other parts of Africa between
a colonial power and a militant nationalist movement whose leaders
had been imprisoned. Those were black versus white negotiations
for black independence; these would be negotiations for a common
white and black purpose. It would, therefore, be as unnecessary as
it would be fatal to appoint as negotiators what Africans aptly call
'good boys' instead of leaders designated by their own people.

Once there is preliminary agreement on possible regions, the next
step would be an inter-regional conference and a number of inter-
regional committees. Techniques for this form of consultation, too,
are well known and inter-provincial committees that might serve
as models are already in existence. There is no need to go into any
details here. Once some sort of finality had been reached within the
RSA, negotiations with Lesotho, Botswana, and Swaziland could
begin. Though the first steps might have to be taken officially by the
South African Government, it would probably be advisable to conduct subsequent negotiations as between the proposed regions within
the RSA and the independent states—that is, not between these
states and the RSA as a unit. Here, too, there are existing models
in the form of consultative committees, such as the one set up to
watch the working of the customs agreement, and of considerable
non-official liaison in banking and other business or industrial undertakings. There are also joint committees of the three states that deal
with common problems. Such negotiations would be facilitated by
the fact that many of the senior officials in Lesotho, Botswana, and
Swaziland are men and women who received most of their training
in the RSA and still have strong cultural and family relations with it.

At some early point in the move to federation there would have to be consultation with the UN. This is not only desirable but necessary in order to break the deadlock over Namibia, to secure the general blessing of world opinion as focused at the UN, and thus to set at rest the fears of the smaller independent states as well as of other countries in Africa and beyond that might see federation as a mask for the expansion of white dominion. In this vitally important and delicate matter it is the RSA Government that would have to take the lead as, indeed, it would have to do if federation is ever to come about. The task which white leaders would take upon themselves would be onerous as well as delicate. In order to persuade Africa and the world of the genuineness and merits of federation they would have to secure the support of the leaders of their dependent Bantustans and of all their non-white subjects even to the extent, as I suggested earlier, of recognizing leaders of what are at present called subversive organizations. In trying to fulfil this task they would find that they were able to draw on a fund of international goodwill and the diplomatic support and advice of most of the major powers, more particularly of the USA, Great Britain, France, India, and Pakistan, and of some of the independent African states who are anxious to see a peaceful arrangement in southern Africa.

At all stages of the protracted negotiations, whether within the RSA or in the more general context, there would be hard bargaining. There could, of course, be no bargaining over civil rights or individual liberty or racial discrimination, but there would be over economic matters. Each region would have economic assets—minerals, the headwaters of a river, a good harbour, well developed transport, strong industrial infra-structure, fruitful soil; and each region would have economic needs—better transport, water and power, more developed industrial infra-structure, access to a harbour. Each region would naturally try to bargain for the most favourable financial arrangements—to get a good share of the national cake.

One need not assume that such bargaining would be on the basis that each region would act solely for its own advantage. In the first place, if there is any desire at all for federation there will be at least a willingness to seek a common southern African good rather than a purely regional one—a realization that what is for the general advantage will also be for the regional good. In the second place, regions that might be tempted to extract the utmost out of the process of partition/federation and federation would be deterred by the fact that, to use a colloquial expression, no one can ever be quite sure how the cookie will crumble. There would be an incentive to pull together and much bargaining would take place not in order to gain an unfair advantage but to ensure that the general interests of the people whom the bargainers represent are safeguarded on a *quid pro quo* basis, so that no region would be worse off than before and could, presumably, expect to be better off.

For federation to have any hope of coming to fruition, public opinion would have to be considered at all stages. This certainly does not mean that all debates should be in public or that hundreds of technical details should be submitted to popular vote. It does mean, however, that at no stage should the public be kept in ignorance. But more than that, it would probably have to be prepared and educated, both for the very conception of federation and for its final form. It was shown in an earlier chapter that the word 'federation' has acquired unfortunate connotations in and about Africa; and that the history of white conquest over southern Africa has left memories of ancient wrongs in people's minds. The idea of federation between former enemies, between ruler and ruled, would have to be made palatable to both ruler and ruled. After that, the task of convincing the public that a particular form of federation is desirable would not be difficult and would depend mainly on the leaders.

Methods of doing these things would naturally differ from region to region. The Transkei and Swaziland, for instance, would probably adopt different methods from those employed by, say, a mainly white area in the RSA. But the technique of informing public opinion honestly, and thus educating it, are by now fairly well known, no matter which race constitutes the public. An impartial broadcasting and television system would play a great part in this, as it did in Britain over the question of joining the Common Market. So, naturally, would the press.

When all the talks, the committees, the conferences and conventions had done their work and federal and regional constitutions had been produced, they would have been agreed upon by the representatives of all the regions. There would then remain one final question: should these be submitted to a popular vote by referendum? If we were dealing with sovereign states only there would be much to be said for leaving the final decision to a national convention of elected representatives. The regions in the RSA, however, would only become autonomous after partition/federation and since there would in any case have to be two conventions, the one to agree to partition/ federation of the RSA and the final one to agree to a wider federation, it might be advisable for the RSA to hold a referendum in which all adults were asked to approve or reject partition/federation. If the majority agreed, the autonomous regions would come into being at a date to be fixed. The independent states of Lesotho, Swaziland, and Botswana would naturally decide for themselves whether to hold a referendum. It was suggested in a previous chapter that it would be possible to arrange that partition/federation and federation should come into existence simultaneously; but if the above procedure is carried out logically the final convention of fifteen autonomous regions might have to take place only after the federation of the RSA had been established.

These details, however, are like much else that has been said in the previous pages of this chapter—matters for decision at the right time by those most concerned. They are introduced here merely to add some concreteness to the discussion. The techniques and the pitfalls of constitution-making and constitutional conferences are, by 1970, well known and there are plenty of precedents available. These would obviously be closely studied by those who have to arrange and take part in the consultations and conferences, and there is no need to say anything more about them here. What has been said may enable readers to form a general picture of how the territories of southern Africa could, if they wished, move from their present constitutional arrangements to new ones.

11

CONCLUSION

Is a federation of southern Africa, such as has been suggested in previous chapters, desirable and is it possible? The answers to these two questions must be conditional and based on a number of assumptions.

Different people expect different things from federation. Lord Carnarvon, quite simply, wanted to combine the white people of two British colonies and two Boer republics. Cecil Rhodes had visions of an expanded British Empire in which the Anglo-Saxons were to inherit the earth and rule it beneficently. Smuts thought of an ill-defined southern Africa in holistic terms, and in a more modern idiom Verwoerd spoke about a commonwealth in southern Africa. All these conceptions of federation were based on white supremacy and were essentially imperial in conception. It is, of course, not necessary for federation, if it becomes imperial, to be based on the supremacy of one particular race. There are instances in Africa and India of what were in effect imperial federations that were based on the domination of one tribe or kingdom over states of the same race. It is, however, not a question of racial supremacy. If the object of any proposed federation is to secure the supremacy of one group over others, then it is not only undesirable but, in terms of the modern world, not possible in the long run.

There are other people who believe in the political magic of a constitution and expect it to perform miracles. If the body politic shows evidence of disharmony and imbalance, change the constitution. If there are political and racial evils under a unitary system, change to a federation and all will be well. In the eyes of such people federation is a panacea for all ills. This simplistic view is not imperialist but it is equally undesirable, because federation, based on such false hopes, will end in disappointment and, possibly, greater disharmony and imbalance than before. Negotiations for federation based on such expectations will in any case not get very far in southern Africa or elsewhere. There is nothing magical about federalism.

Franz L. Neumann has pointed out that a federal state is not necessarily more favourable to political and civil freedom than a unitary
state. There is no inherent connection between federalism and
democracy. But there are political goals that can be attained only
through federalism.[1]

Carl J. Friedrich, in *Trends of Federalism in Theory and Practice*,
says that federalism is perhaps 'primarily the process by which a
number of separate political communities enter into an arrangement
for working out solutions, adopting joint policies, and making
joint decisions on joint problems, and, conversely, also the process
by which a unitary community becomes differentiated into a federally
organized whole'.[2] Later in the same book he says that federalism
can provide channels for inter-group communication. It affords
both integrative and differentiating forces room to operate in. And
finally, speaking about the constitution of the USA, he says that
federalism is (or should be) highly pragmatic. The Founding Fathers
in the USA avoided all insistence on 'agreement on fundamentals'
and such-like rigidly doctrinaire formulas. To behave federally is
to proceed in the spirit of compromise and accommodation. The
American constitution is moulded in the knowledge 'that there are
many rooms in the house that federation builds'.

Thinking along these lines, the peoples of southern Africa—and
in practice, to begin with, this means their leaders—may desire a
peaceful coexistence to which existing constitutional arrangements
are not conducive. They might then turn to federation as a practical
method of securing what they want. Negotiations undertaken to
that end will not be disguised moves to promote the domination of
one group; nor will they be vitiated by hopes of political miracles—
of, for instance, getting rid of racial prejudice by a change of constitution. They will be undertaken in the severely practical spirit of
trying to secure union, not unity, and the negotiators will face all
that is involved in this rather than disguise motives or sweep un-
comfortable facts under the conference room carpet. If such practical
negotiations were to succeed, they would end in avoiding the disaster
of race war or stagnation in southern Africa. Federalism of this
kind is desirable and, indeed, it is one of the conditions of its
possibility that it must be so desired.

This precondition for federation holds certain assumptions. If the

[1] Macmahon, ed., *Federalism—Mature and Emergent*, Chapter 3.
[2] Carl J. Friedrich, op. cit., pp. 5–8.

people of southern Africa should in time want a federation because it appears to be a practical method of securing peaceful coexistence, it must be assumed that they have become aware that under present constitutional arrangements they have failed to promote such coexistence. In other words, they must have come to believe that the policies that have been hitherto pursued might possibly be modified under a different kind of constitution. This applies to all the people of southern Africa but in a very special manner to the whites, for the simple and sufficient reason that the policies are of their making. The whites are justified in wishing to prevent their culture and standards from being submerged, and so far the only policy that they have been able to forge to this end has been apartheid. If the whites want a federation, therefore, one must assume that they have become aware that the present racial policies cannot succeed and that alternative policies have a better chance of doing so under a federal constitution.

For federation to have become generally desirable one must assume that southern Africans see how it could favour policies that would advance their common interests. In the nature of things, once more, the whites in particular would have come to realize the distinction between their desires and their interests in relation to the rest of the population. They desire to retain their culture and their privileged standard of living and have decided that their desires are paramount, without pausing to inquire whether their interests might not be better served if the interests of the whole population were paramount rather than the desires of one group. The interests of any one group in a society are never paramount; and when the desires of such a group are elevated and become regarded as interests, group supremacy results. If the group happens to be of a race that is different from the rest of the society, racial supremacy results.

A second assumption in this connection is that the whites of southern Africa have come to realize the distinction between surrendering and sharing power. This distinction was made in Chapter 7 but it is worth repeating briefly. In general it is true that no class ever surrenders power except as the result of violence, though twentieth-century decolonization might be regarded as, at least, a partial exception. But classes have before now decided to share power with other classes—possibly on the basis of 'if you can't beat 'em, join 'em'. Such classes have been fully aware of what sharing power means, and one must assume that, if the whites of southern

Africa were prepared to share power, they too would have calculated the risks and gains—would have weighed the price of federation against the price of apartheid.

The few previous paragraphs applied chiefly to whites, but assumptions will have to be made about non-whites if we are to say whether federation is desirable and possible. If non-whites are not effectively consulted, or if their opinions are ignored, and they are dragged into a federation of southern Africa either without their positive consent or against their will, federation would be highly undesirable. This implies the assumption that non-whites are convinced of the advantages of federation and are assured that the whites are genuine in their desire to follow new policies through a federal constitution. One must assume, too, that no non-white leaders are foolish enough to welcome a race war for the sake of exacting revenge on the white man. This is an assumption that can no longer be confidently made about some of the more extreme anti-racists in Europe and America who often appear to want a revolution in South Africa because this will give white South Africans a taste of their own medicine. They may or may not have paused to consider that a non-white revolution in South Africa has little chance of success and that there is every chance that it would turn into an equally unsuccessful southern African race war. From there, no one can predict what will happen except useless bloodshed and widespread misery.

These presumptions and conditions, then, must qualify any answer that can be given about the desirability and possibility of a southern African federation. The presumptions need not be totally valid, and it would be foolish to refrain from taking steps towards federation on the grounds that all the conditions have not been fulfilled. Life is not like that. If the conditions are largely fulfilled and the presumptions for the most part valid, federation would be both desirable and possible; and it is probable that federation would itself help to fulfil the conditions on which it should be based. But if whites cling to discriminatory policies, and non-whites cannot rid themselves of the fear that federation means apartheid writ large, there is little more that can usefully be said except by way of preparing for disaster and, after that, to do what mankind has always done: rebuild. When one ponders the disasters, however, it becomes all the more urgent to negotiate before rather than after. It becomes all the more imperative for white and non-white to ask whether federation does not offer hope—not of a quick solution of problems, but of dissolving the prejudices and fears that create the problems. Constitutions and laws cannot abolish prejudice in the human mind, but they can help to create the climate in which the fears that feed on prejudice are more easily dissolved. This is what a federation of southern Africa, built on strong realistic foundations and constructed on practical lines, could do.

INDEX

African National Congress, 56, 131
Anglo-Boer War, 27, 33
Angola, 8, 54, 59, 62, 119
Apartheid, *see* Race policies
Asians, 5, 6, 7, 8, 69, 73, 74, 130
Atomic Energy Commission, 9
Australia, 16, 21, 27, 30, 110 n.

Bamangwato, 42
Bantustans, 7, 50, 56 et seq., 69, 76, 79, 80, 81, 85, and federation, Chap. 6 *passim*, 91, 106, 108, 109, 112, 113, 118
Bapedi, 36, 73
Basutoland, *see* Lesotho
Bechuanaland, *see* Botswana
Berry, Bisset, 33
Bondelzwarts, 60
Botha, Louis, 31
Botswana, 8, 26, 27, 35, 40, Chap. 4 *passim*, 57, 60, 62, 66, 70; and federation, Chap. 7 *passim*, 94, 97, 103, Chap. 9 *passim*, 124, 125, 128, 130 et seq.
Britain, 2, 4, 18, 19, 20, 26 et seq., 110 n., 132

Cabora Bassa, 107, 110
Caledon River, 52
Cameron, Donald, 37
Canada, 10, 17, 27, 30, 31, 67, 110 n.
Cape Colony or province, 26 et seq., 41, 47, 59, 68, 69, 102, 104, 125
Cape Coloured, *see* Coloured
Caprivi Strip, 54
Carnarvon, Lord, 27
Central African Federation, 18, 24, 62, 94, 127
China, 120
Colonialism, 4, 5, 6, 7, 20
Coloured, 5, 6, 7, 8, 11, 28, 69, 73, 74, 76, 130
Commonwealth, 56, 57, 62, 63, 84 et seq., 111
Communism, 120 et seq.

Damara, 92

Defence, 16, 18, 32, 33, 53, 54, 60–4, 97, 118 et seq.
de Villiers, Sir Henry, 31
Dicey, 14

Ethiopia, 9, 47
European Common Market, 110
Exchange Control Act (British), 110 n.

Fagan Commission, 89
Federation, general theory, Chap. 2 *passim*
Federation, southern Africa, Chaps. 6–11 *passim*
Food and Agricultural Organization, 9
France (and French), 4, 8, 22, 119, 132
Friedrich, Carl J., 136
Fugard, Athol, 11, 11 n.

Gaberones, 53
Germany, 2, 9, 26, 35, 45, 46, 92
Gordimer, Nadine, 11
Great Trek, 27
Grey, Sir George, 27
Group Areas Act, 102

Havenga, N. J., 108
Herero, 91, 92
Hertzog, J. B. M, 42, 105 n.
Hicks, U. K., 16 n.
High Commission Territories, *see* Botswana, Lesotho, Swaziland
Hofmeyr, J. H., 33
Holland, 8

Immorality Act, 102, 103 n.
India, 8, 116, 119, 132
International Court of Justice, 9, 10 n., 47
International Labour Organization, 9
International Monetary Fund, 9

Jameson, Sir L. S., 27
Jonathan, Chief Leabua, 40

Khama, Sir Seretse, 48–50, 53, 58, 83
Kunene River, 107